BAB BALLADS AND SAVOY SONGS

LECTOR HOUSE PUBLIC DOMAIN WORKS

This book is a result of an effort made by Lector House towards making a contribution to the preservation and repair of original classic literature. The original text is in the public domain in the United States of America, and possibly other countries depending upon their specific copyright laws.

In an attempt to preserve, improve and recreate the original content, certain conventional norms with regard to typographical mistakes, hyphenations, punctuations and/or other related subject matters, have been corrected upon our consideration. However, few such imperfections might not have been rectified as they were inherited and preserved from the original content to maintain the authenticity and construct, relevant to the work. The work might contain a few prior copyright references which have been retained, wherever considered relevant to the part of the construct. We believe that this work holds historical, cultural and/or intellectual importance in the literary works community, therefore despite the oddities, we accounted the work for print as a part of our continuing effort towards preservation of literary work and our contribution towards the development of the society as a whole, driven by our beliefs.

We are grateful to our readers for putting their faith in us and accepting our imperfections with regard to preservation of the historical content. We shall strive hard to meet up to the expectations to improve further to provide an enriching reading experience.

Though, we conduct extensive research in ascertaining the status of copyright before redeveloping a version of the content, in rare cases, a classic work might be incorrectly marked as not-in-copyright. In such cases, if you are the copyright holder, then kindly contact us or write to us, and we shall get back to you with an immediate course of action.

HAPPY READING!

BAB BALLADS AND SAVOY SONGS

WILLIAM SCHWENCK GILBERT

ISBN: 978-93-90294-28-2

Published: -

© 2020
LECTOR HOUSE LLP

LECTOR HOUSE LLP
E-MAIL: lectorpublishing@gmail.com

BAB BALLADS AND SAVOY SONGS

BY

W. S. GILBERT

CONTENTS

Page

THE BAB BALLADS.

- THE YARN OF THE "NANCY BELL." 1
- CAPTAIN REECE.. 4
- THE BISHOP AND THE BUSMAN.. 7
- THE FOLLY OF BROWN. 9
- THE THREE KINGS OF CHICKERABOO. 12
- THE BISHOP OF RUM-TI-FOO. 14
- TO THE TERRESTRIAL GLOBE. 17
- GENERAL JOHN. 18
- SIR GUY THE CRUSADER. 20
- KING BORRIA BUNGALEE BOO. 22
- THE TROUBADOUR.. 26
- THE FORCE OF ARGUMENT.. 29
- ONLY A DANCING GIRL.. 32
- THE SENSATION CAPTAIN. 34
- THE PERIWINKLE GIRL. 37
- BOB POLTER. 40
- GENTLE ALICE BROWN. 43
- BEN ALLAH ACHMET; 46

SONGS OF A SAVOYARD

CONTENTS

- THE ENGLISHMAN..50
- THE DISAGREEABLE MAN...............................51
- THE MODERN MAJOR-GENERAL.........................52
- THE HEAVY DRAGOON..................................54
- ONLY ROSES!...56
- THEY'LL NONE OF 'EM BE MISSED.....................57
- THE POLICEMAN'S LOT.................................58
- AN APPEAL...60
- EHEU FUGACES—!......................................61
- A RECIPE..62
- THE FIRST LORD'S SONG...............................63
- WHEN A MERRY MAIDEN MARRIES......................64
- THE SUICIDE'S GRAVE..................................65
- HE AND SHE..66
- THE LORD CHANCELLOR'S SONG........................68
- WILLOW WALY!...70
- THE USHER'S CHARGE..................................71
- KING GOODHEART......................................72
- THE TANGLED SKEIN...................................74
- GIRL GRADUATES.......................................75
- THE APE AND THE LADY................................77
- SANS SOUCI..78
- THE BRITISH TAR.......................................79
- THE COMING BYE AND BYE.............................80
- THE SORCERER'S SONG.................................82
- SPECULATION..84
- THE DUKE OF PLAZA-TORO.............................85
- THE REWARD OF MERIT.................................87

- WHEN I FIRST PUT THIS UNIFORM ON.. 88
- SAID I TO MYSELF, SAID I. 89
- THE FAMILY FOOL. 91
- THE PHILOSOPHIC PILL.. 93
- THE CONTEMPLATIVE SENTRY. 94
- SORRY HER LOT.. 95
- THE JUDGE'S SONG.. 96
- TRUE DIFFIDENCE. 98
- THE HIGHLY RESPECTABLE GONDOLIER. 99
- DON'T FORGET. 101
- THE DARNED MOUNSEER. 103
- THE HUMANE MIKADO.. 105
- THE HOUSE OF PEERS. 107
- THE ÆSTHETE.. 108
- PROPER PRIDE.. 110
- THE BAFFLED GRUMBLER. 111
- THE WORKING MONARCH.. .113
- THE ROVER'S APOLOGY.. 115
- WOULD YOU KNOW?. 116
- THE MAGNET AND THE CHURN. 117
- BRAID THE RAVEN HAIR. 119
- IS LIFE A BOON? 120
- A MIRAGE.. 121
- A MERRY MADRIGAL. 123
- THE LOVE-SICK BOY. 124

THE BAB BALLADS.

THE YARN OF THE "NANCY BELL."

'Twas on the shores that round our coast
From Deal to Ramsgate span,
That I found alone, on a piece of stone,
An elderly naval man.

His hair was weedy, his beard was long,
And weedy and long was he,
And I heard this wight on the shore recite,
In a singular minor key:

"Oh, I am a cook and a captain bold,
And the mate of the *Nancy* brig,
And a bo'sun tight, and a midshipmite,
And the crew of the captain's gig."

And he shook his fists and he tore his hair,
Till I really felt afraid;
For I couldn't help thinking the man had been drinking,
And so I simply said:

"Oh, elderly man it's little I know
Of the duties of men of the sea,
And I'll eat my hand if I understand
How you can possibly be

"At once a cook, and a captain bold,
And the mate of the *Nancy* brig,
And a bo'sun tight and a midshipmite,
And the crew of the captain's gig."

Then he gave a hitch to his trousers, which
Is a trick all seamen larn,
And having got rid of a thumping quid,
He spun this painful yarn:

"'Twas in the good ship *Nancy Bell*
That we sailed to the Indian sea,
And there on a reef we come to grief,
Which has often occurred to me.

"And pretty nigh all o' the crew was drowned
(There was seventy-seven o' soul),
And only ten of the *Nancy's* men

Said 'Here!' to the muster roll.

"There was me and the cook and the captain bold,
And the mate of the *Nancy* brig,
And the bo'sun tight and a midshipmite,
And the crew of the captain's gig.

"For a month we'd neither wittles nor drink,
Till a-hungry we did feel,
So, we drawed a lot, and, accordin' shot
The captain for our meal.

"The next lot fell to the *Nancy's* mate,
And a delicate dish he made;
Then our appetite with the midshipmite
We seven survivors stayed.

"And then we murdered the bo'sun tight,
And he much resembled pig;
Then we wittled free, did the cook and me,
On the crew of the captain's gig.

"Then only the cook and me was left,
And the delicate question, 'Which
Of us two goes to the kettle?' arose,
And we argued it out as sich.

"For I loved that cook as a brother, I did,
And the cook he worshipped me;
But we'd both be blowed if we'd either be stowed
In the other chap's hold, you see.

"'I'll be eat if you dines off me,' says Tom,
'Yes, that,' says I, 'you'll be,' —
'I'm boiled if I die, my friend,' quoth I,
And 'Exactly so,' quoth he.

"Says he, 'Dear James, to murder me
Were a foolish thing to do,
For don't you see that you can't cook *me*,
While I can—and will—cook *you!*'

"So, he boils the water, and takes the salt
And the pepper in portions true
(Which he never forgot), and some chopped shalot,
And some sage and parsley too.

"'Come here,' says he, with a proper pride,
Which his smiling features tell,
"'T will soothing be if I let you see,
How extremely nice you'll smell,'

"And he stirred it round and round and round,

And he sniffed the foaming froth;
When I ups with his heels, and smothers his squeals
In the scum of the boiling broth.

"And I eat that cook in a week or less,
And—as I eating be
The last of his chops, why I almost drops,
For a wessel in sight I see.

"And I never larf, and I never smile,
And I never lark nor play,
But I sit and croak, and a single joke
I have—which is to say:

"Oh, I am a cook and a captain bold,
And the mate of the *Nancy* brig,
And a bo'sun tight, and a midshipmite,
And the crew of the captain's gig!"

CAPTAIN REECE.

Of all the ships upon the blue,
No ship contained a better crew
Than that of worthy Captain Reece,
Commanding of *The Mantelpiece*.

He was adored by all his men,
For worthy Captain Reece, R.N.,
Did all that lay within him to
Promote the comfort of his crew.

If ever they were dull or sad,
Their captain danced to them like mad,
Or told, to make the time pass by,
Droll legends of his infancy.

A feather bed had every man,
Warm slippers and hot-water can,
Brown windsor from the captain's store,
A valet, too, to every four.

Did they with thirst in summer burn?
Lo, seltzogenes at every turn.
And on all very sultry days
Cream ices handed round on trays.

Then currant wine and ginger pops
Stood handily on all the "tops:"
And, also, with amusement rife,
A "Zoetrope, or Wheel of Life."

New volumes came across the sea
From Mister Mudie's libraree;
The Times and *Saturday Review*
Beguiled the leisure of the crew.

Kind-hearted Captain Reece, R.N.,
Was quite devoted to his men;
In point of fact, good Captain Reece
Beatified *The Mantelpiece*.

One summer eve, at half-past ten,
He said (addressing all his men):
"Come, tell me, please, what I can do

To please and gratify my crew.

"By any reasonable plan
I'll make you happy if I can;
My own convenience count as *nil*;
It is my duty, and I will."

Then up and answered William Lee,
(The kindly captain's coxswain he,
A nervous, shy, low-spoken man)
He cleared his throat and thus began:

"You have a daughter, Captain Reece,
Ten female cousins and a niece,
A ma, if what I'm told is true,
Six sisters, and an aunt or two.

"Now, somehow, sir, it seems to me,
More friendly-like we all should be.
If you united of 'em to
Unmarried members of the crew.

"If you'd ameliorate our life,
Let each select from them a wife;
And as for nervous me, old pal,
Give me your own enchanting gal!"

Good Captain Reece, that worthy man,
Debated on his coxswain's plan:
"I quite agree," he said. "O Bill;
It is my duty, and I will.

"My daughter, that enchanting gurl,
has just been promised to an earl,
And all my other familee
To peers of various degree.

"But what are dukes and viscounts to
The happiness of all my crew?
The word I gave you I'll fulfil;
It is my duty, and I will.

"As you desire it shall befall,
I'll settle thousands on you all,
And I shall be, despite my hoard,
The only bachelor on board."

The boatswain of *The Mantelpiece*,
He blushed and spoke to Captain Reece:
"I beg your honor's leave," he said,
"If you wish to go and wed,

"I have a widowed mother who

Would be the very thing for you—
She long has loved you from afar,
She washes for you, Captain R."

The captain saw the dame that day—
Addressed her in his playful way—
"And did it want a wedding ring?
It was a tempting ickle sing!

"Well, well, the chaplain I will seek,
We'll all be married this day week—
At yonder church upon the hill;
It is my duty, and I will!"

The sisters, cousins, aunts, and niece,
And widowed ma of Captain Reece,
Attended there as they were bid;
It was their duty, and they did.

THE BISHOP AND THE BUSMAN.

It was a Bishop bold,
And London was his see,
He was short and stout and round about,
And zealous as could be.

It also was a Jew,
Who drove a Putney bus—
For flesh of swine however fine
He did not care a cuss.

His name was Hash Baz Ben,
And Jedediah too,
And Solomon and Zabulon—
This bus-directing Jew.

The Bishop said, said he,
"I'll see what I can do
To Christianize and make you wise,
You poor benighted Jew."

So every blessed day
That bus he rode outside,
From Fulham town, both up and down,
And loudly thus he cried:—

"His name is Hash Baz Ben,
And Jedediah too,
And Solomon and Zabulon—
This bus-directing Jew."

At first the busman smiled,
And rather liked the fun—
He merely smiled, that Hebrew child,
And said, "Eccentric one!"

And gay young dogs would wait
To see the bus go by
(These gay young dogs in striking togs)
To hear the Bishop cry:—

"Observe his grisly beard,
His race it clearly shows,
He sticks no fork in ham or pork:—

Observe, my friends, his nose.

"His name is Hash Baz Ben,
And Jedediah too,
And Solomon and Zabulon—
This bus-directing Jew."

But though at first amused,
Yet after seven years,
This Hebrew child got awful riled,
And busted into tears.

He really almost feared
To leave his poor abode,
His nose, and name, and beard became
A byword on that road.

At length he swore an oath,
The reason he would know—
"I'll call and see why ever he
Does persecute me so."

The good old bishop sat
On his ancestral chair,
The busman came, sent up his name,
And laid his grievance bare.

"Benighted Jew," he said,
(And chuckled loud with joy)
"Be Christian you, instead of Jew—
Become a Christian boy.

"I'll ne'er annoy you more."
"Indeed?" replied the Jew.
"Shall I be freed?" "You will, indeed!"
Then "Done!" said he, "with you!"

The organ which, in man,
Between the eyebrows grows,
Fell from his face, and in its place,
He found a Christian nose.

His tangled Hebrew beard,
Which to his waist came down,
Was now a pair of whiskers fair—
His name, Adolphus Brown.

He wedded in a year,
That prelate's daughter Jane;
He's grown quite fair—has auburn hair—
His wife is far from plain.

THE FOLLY OF BROWN.
BY A GENERAL AGENT.

I knew a boor—a clownish card,
(His only friends were pigs and cows and
The poultry of a small farmyard)
Who came into two hundred thousand.

Good fortune worked no change in Brown,
Though she's a mighty social chymist:
He was a clown—and by a clown
I do not mean a pantomimist.

It left him quiet, calm, and cool,
Though hardly knowing what a crown was—
You can't imagine what a fool
Poor rich, uneducated Brown was!

He scouted all who wished to come
And give him monetary schooling;
And I propose to give you some
Idea of his insensate fooling.

I formed a company or two—
(Of course I don't know what the rest meant,
I formed them solely with a view
To help him to a sound investment).

Their objects were—their only cares—
To justify their Boards in showing
A handsome dividend on shares,
And keep their good promoter going.

But no—the lout prefers his brass,
Though shares at par I freely proffer:
Yes—will it be believed?—the ass
Declines, with thanks, my well-meant offer!

He added, with a bumpkin's grin,
(A weakly intellect denoting)
He'd rather not invest it in
A company of my promoting!

"You have two hundred 'thou' or more,"

Said I. "You'll waste it, lose it, lend it.
Come, take my furnished second floor,
I'll gladly show you how to spend it."

But will it be believed that he,
With grin upon his face of poppy,
Declined my aid, while thanking me
For what he called my "philanthroppy?"

Some blind, suspicious fools rejoice
In doubting friends who wouldn't harm them;
They will not hear the charmer's voice,
However wisely he may charm them.

I showed him that his coat, all dust,
Top boots and cords provoked compassion,
And proved that men of station must
Conform to the decrees of fashion.

I showed him where to buy his hat,
To coat him, trouser him, and boot him;
But no—he wouldn't hear of that—
"He didn't think the style would suit him!"

I offered him a country seat,
And made no end of an oration;
I made it certainly complete,
And introduced the deputation.

But no—the clown my prospects blights—
(The worth of birth it surely teaches!)
"Why should I want to spend my nights
In Parliament, a-making speeches?

"I haven't never been to school—
I ain't had not no eddication—
And I should surely be a fool
To publish that to all the nation!"

I offered him a trotting horse—
No hack had ever trotted faster—
I also offered him, of course,
A rare and curious "old Master."

I offered to procure him weeds—
Wines fit for one in his position—
But, though an ass in all his deeds,
He'd learnt the meaning of "commission."

He called me "thief" the other day,
And daily from his door he thrusts me;
Much more of this, and soon I may
Begin to think that Brown mistrusts me.

THE FOLLY OF BROWN.

So deaf to all sound Reason's rule
This poor uneducated clown is,
You cannot fancy what a fool
Poor rich uneducated Brown is.

THE THREE KINGS OF CHICKERABOO.

There were three niggers of Chickeraboo—
Pacifico, Bang-Bang, Popchop—who
Exclaimed, one terribly sultry day,
"Oh, let's be kings in a humble way."

The first was a highly-accomplished "bones,"
The next elicited banjo tones,
The third was a quiet, retiring chap,
Who danced an excellent break-down "flap."

"We niggers," said they, "have formed a plan
By which, whenever we like, we can
Extemporize islands near the beach,
And then we'll collar an island each.

"Three casks, from somebody else's stores,
Shall rep-per-esent our island shores,
Their sides the ocean wide shall lave,
Their heads just topping the briny wave.

"Great Britain's navy scours the sea,
And everywhere her ships they be,
She'll recognize our rank, perhaps,
When she discovers we're Royal Chaps.

"If to her skirts you want to cling,
It's quite sufficient that you're a king:
She does not push inquiry far
To learn what sort of king you are."

A ship of several thousand tons,
And mounting seventy-something guns,
Ploughed, every year, the ocean blue,
Discovering kings and countries new.

The brave Rear-Admiral Bailey Pip,
Commanding that superior ship,
Perceived one day, his glasses through,
The kings that came from Chickeraboo.

"Dear eyes!" said Admiral Pip, "I see
Three flourishing islands on our lee.
And, bless me! most extror'nary thing!

THE THREE KINGS OF CHICKERABOO.

On every island stands a king!

"Come, lower the Admiral's gig," he cried,
"And over the dancing waves I'll glide;
That low obeisance I may do
To those three kings of Chickeraboo!"

The admiral pulled to the islands three;
The kings saluted him gracious*lee*.
The admiral, pleased at his welcome warm,
Pulled out a printed Alliance form.

"Your Majesty, sign me this, I pray—
I come in a friendly kind of way—
I come, if you please, with the best intents,
And Queen Victoria's compliments."

The kings were pleased as they well could be;
The most retiring of all the three,
In a "cellar-flap" to his joy gave vent
With a banjo-bones accompaniment.

The great Rear-Admiral Bailey Pip
Embarked on board his jolly big ship,
Blue Peter flew from his lofty fore,
And off he sailed to his native shore.

Admiral Pip directly went
To the Lord at the head of the Government,
Who made him, by a stroke of a quill,
Baron de Pippe, of Pippetonneville.

The College of Heralds permission yield
That he should quarter upon his shield
Three islands, *vert*, on a field of blue,
With the pregnant motto "Chickeraboo."

Ambassadors, yes, and attaches, too,
Are going to sail for Chickeraboo,
And, see, on the good ship's crowded deck,
A bishop, who's going out there on spec.

And let us all hope that blissful things
May come of alliance with darkey kings.
Oh, may we never, whatever we do,
Declare a war with Chickeraboo!

THE BISHOP OF RUM-TI-FOO.

From east and south the holy clan
Of bishops gathered, to a man;
To synod, called Pan-Anglican;
In flocking crowds they came.
Among them was a Bishop, who
Had lately been appointed to
The balmy isle of Rum-ti-Foo,
And Peter was his name.

His people—twenty-three in sum—
They played the eloquent tum-tum
And lived on scalps served up in rum—
The only sauce they knew,
When, first good Bishop Peter came
(For Peter was that Bishop's name),
To humor them, he did the same
As they of Rum-ti-Foo.

His flock, I've often heard him tell,
(His name was Peter) loved him well,

THE BISHOP OF RUM-TI-FOO.

And summoned by the sound of bell,
In crowds together came.
"Oh, massa, why you go away?
Oh, Massa Peter, please to stay."
(They called him Peter, people say,
Because it was his name.)

He told them all good boys to be,
And sailed away across the sea.
At London Bridge that Bishop he
Arrived one Tuesday night—
And as that night he homeward strode
To his Pan-Anglican abode,
He passed along the Borough Road
And saw a gruesome sight.

He saw a crowd assembled round
A person dancing on the ground,
Who straight began to leap and bound
With all his might and main.
To see that dancing man he stopped.
Who twirled and wriggled, skipped and hopped,
Then down incontinently dropped,
And then sprang up again.

The Bishop chuckled at the sight,
"This style of dancing would delight
A simple Rum-ti-Foozle-ite.
I'll learn it, if I can,
To please the tribe when I get back."
He begged the man to teach his knack.
"Right Reverend Sir, in half a crack,"
Replied that dancing man.

The dancing man he worked away
And taught the Bishop every day—
The dancer skipped like any fay—
Good Peter did the same.
The Bishop buckled to his task
With *battements*, cuts, and *pas de basque*
(I'll tell you, if you care to ask,
That Peter was his name).

"Come, walk like this," the dancer said,
"Stick out your toes—stick in your head.
Stalk on with quick, galvanic tread—
Your fingers thus extend;
The attitude's considered quaint,"
The weary Bishop, feeling faint,

Replied, "I do not say it ain't,
But 'Time!' my Christian friend!"

"We now proceed to something new—
Dance as the Paynes and Lauris do,
Like this—one, two—one, two—one, two."
The Bishop, never proud,
But in an overwhelming heat
(His name was Peter, I repeat),
Performed the Payne and Lauri feat,
And puffed his thanks aloud.

Another game the dancer planned—
"Just take your ankle in your hand,
And try, my lord, if you can stand—
Your body stiff and stark.
If, when revisiting your see,
You learnt to hop on shore—like me—
The novelty must striking be,
And must excite remark."

"No," said the worthy Bishop, "No;
That is a length to which, I trow,
Colonial Bishops cannot go.
You may express surprise
At finding Bishops deal in pride—
But, if that trick I ever tried,
I should appear undignified
In Rum-ti-Foozle's eyes.

"The islanders of Rum-ti-Foo
Are well-conducted persons, who
Approve a joke as much as you,
And laugh at it as such;
But if they saw their Bishop land,
His leg supported in his hand,
The joke they wouldn't understand—
'Twould pain them very much!"

TO THE TERRESTRIAL GLOBE.
BY A MISERABLE WRETCH.

Roll on, thou ball, roll on!
Through pathless realms of Space
Roll on!
What, though I'm in a sorry case?
What, though I cannot meet my bills?
What, though I suffer toothache's ills?
What, though I swallow countless pills?
Never *you* mind!
Roll on!

Roll on, thou ball, roll on!
Through seas of inky air
Roll on!
It's true I've got no shirts to wear;
It's true my butcher's bill is due;
It's true my prospects all look blue—
But don't let that unsettle you!
Never *you* mind!
Roll on!

(It rolls on.)

GENERAL JOHN.

The bravest names for fire and flames,
And all that mortal durst,
Were General John and Private James,
Of the Sixty-seventy-first.

General John was a soldier tried,
A chief of warlike dons;
A haughty stride and a withering pride
Were Major-General John's.

A sneer would play on his martial phiz,
Superior birth to show;
"Pish!" was a favorite word of his,
And he often said "Ho! ho!"

Full-Private James described might be,
As a man of a mournful mind;
No characteristic trait had he
Of any distinctive kind.

From the ranks, one day, cried Private James
"Oh! Major-General John,
I've doubts of our respective names,
My mournful mind upon.

"A glimmering thought occurs to me,
(Its source I can't unearth)
But I've a kind of notion we
Were cruelly changed at birth.

"I've a strange idea, each other's names
That we have each got on,
Such things have been," said Private James.
"They have!" sneered General John.

"My General John, I swear upon
My oath I think 'tis so" —
"Pish!" proudly sneered his General John,
And he also said "Ho! ho!"

"My General John! my General John!
My General John!" quoth he,
"This aristocratical sneer upon

GENERAL JOHN.

Your face I blush to see!

"No truly great or generous cove
Deserving of them names
Would sneer at a fixed idea that's drove
In the mind of a Private James!"

Said General John, "Upon your claims
No need your breath to waste;
If this is a joke, Full-Private James,
It's a joke of doubtful taste.

"But being a man of doubtless worth,
If you feel certain quite
That we were probably changed at birth,
I'll venture to say you're right."

So General John as Private James
Fell in, parade upon;
And Private James, by change of names,
Was Major-General John.

SIR GUY THE CRUSADER.

Sir Guy was a doughty crusader,
A muscular knight,
Ever ready to fight,
A very determined invader.
And Dickey de Lion's delight.

Lenore was a Saracen maiden,
Brunette, statuesque,
The reverse of grotesque;
Her pa was a bagman at Aden,
Her mother she played in burlesque.

A *coryphee* pretty and loyal.
In amber and red,
The ballet she led;
Her mother performed at the Royal,
Lenore at the Saracen's Head.

Of face and of figure majestic,
She dazzled the cits—
Ecstaticized pits;—
Her troubles were only domestic,
But drove her half out of her wits.

Her father incessantly lashed her,
On water and bread
She was grudgingly fed;
Whenever her father he thrashed her
Her mother sat down on her head.

Guy saw her, and loved her, with reason,
For beauty so bright,
Set him mad with delight;
He purchased a stall for the season
And sat in it every night.

His views were exceedingly proper;
He wanted to wed,
So he called at her shed
And saw her progenitor whop her—
Her mother sit down on her head.

SIR GUY THE CRUSADER.

"So pretty," said he, "and so trusting!
You brute of a dad,
You unprincipled cad,
Your conduct is really disgusting.
Come, come, now, admit it's too bad!

"You're a turbaned old Turk, and malignant;
Your daughter Lenore
I intensely adore
And I cannot help feeling indignant,
A fact that I hinted before.

"To see a fond father employing
A deuce of a knout
For to bang her about.
To a sensitive lover's annoying."
Said the bagman, "Crusader, get out!"

Says Guy, "Shall a warrior laden
With a big spiky knob.
Stand idly and sob.
While a beautiful Saracen maiden
Is whipped by a Saracen snob?

"To London I'll go from my charmer."
Which he did, with his loot
(Seven hats and a flute),
And was nabbed for his Sydenham armor,
At Mr. Ben-Samuel's suit.

Sir Guy he was lodged in the Compter,
Her pa, in a rage,
Died (don't know his age),
His daughter, she married the prompter,
Grew bulky and quitted the stage.

KING BORRIA BUNGALEE BOO.

King Borria Bungalee Boo
Was a man-eating African swell;
His sigh was a hullaballoo,
His whisper a horrible yell—
A horrible, horrible yell!

Four subjects, and all of them male,
To Borria doubled the knee,
They were once on a far larger scale,
But he'd eaten the balance, you see
("Scale" and "balance" is punning, you see.)

There was haughty Pish-Tush-Pooh-Bah,
There was lumbering Doodle-Dum-Deh,
Despairing Alack-a-Dey-Ah,
And good little Tootle-Tum-Teh—

Exemplary Tootle-Tum-Teh.

One day there was grief in the crew,
For they hadn't a morsel of meat,
And Borria Bungalee Boo
Was dying for something to eat—
"Come provide me with something to eat!"

"Alack-a-Dey, famished I feel;
Oh, good little Tootle-Tum-Teh,
Where on earth shall I look for a meal?
For I haven't no dinner to-day!—
Not a morsel of dinner to-day!

"Dear Tootle-Tum, what shall we do?
Come, get us a meal, or in truth,
If you don't we shall have to eat you,
Oh, adorable friend of our youth!
Thou beloved little friend of our youth!"

And he answered, "Oh Bungalee Boo,
For a moment I hope you will wait—
Tippy-Wippity Tol-the-Rol-Loo
Is the queen of a neighboring state—
A remarkably neighboring state.

"Tippy-Wippity Tol-the-Rol-Loo,
She would pickle deliciously cold—
And her four pretty Amazons, too,
Are enticing, and not very old—
Twenty-seven is not very old.

"There is neat little Titty-Fol-Leh,
There is rollicking Tral-the-Ral-Lah,
There is jocular Waggety-Weh.
There is musical Doh-Reh-Mi-Fah—
There's the nightingale Doh-Reh-Mi-Fah!"

So the forces of Bungalee Boo
Marched forth in a terrible row,
And the ladies who fought for Queen Loo
Prepared to encounter the foe—
This dreadful insatiate foe!

But they sharpened no weapons at all,
And they poisoned no arrows—not they!
They made ready to conquer or fall
In a totally different way—
An entirely different way.

With a crimson and pearly-white dye
They endeavored to make themselves fair,

With black they encircled each eye,
And with yellow they painted their hair
(It was wool, but they thought it was hair).

And the forces they met in the field —
And the men of King Borria said,
"Amazonians, immediately yield!"
And their arrows they drew to the head,
Yes, drew them right up to the head.

But jocular Waggety-Weh,
Ogled Doodle-Dum-Deh (which was wrong)
And neat little Titty-Fol-Leh,
Said, "Tootle-Tum, you go along!
You naughty old dear, go along!"

And rollicking Tral-the-Ral-Lah
Tapped Alack-a-Dey-Ah with her fan;
And musical Doh-Reh-Mi-Fah,
Said "Pish, go away, you bad man!
Go away, you delightful young man!"

And the Amazons simpered and sighed,
And they ogled, and giggled, and flushed,
And they opened their pretty eyes wide,
And they chuckled, and flirted, and blushed
(At least, if they could, they'd have blushed).

But haughty Pish-Tush-Pooh-Bah
Said, "Alack-a-Dey, what does this mean?"
And despairing Alack-a-Dey-Ah
Said, "They think us uncommonly green,
Ha! ha! most uncommonly green!"

Even blundering Doodle-Dum-Deh
Was insensible quite to their leers
And said good little Tootle-Tum-Teh,
"It's your blood we desire, pretty dears—
We have come for our dinners, my dears!"

And the Queen of the Amazons fell
To Borria Bungalee Boo,
In a mouthful he gulped, with a yell,
Tippy-Wippity Tol-the-Rol-Loo—
The pretty Queen Tol-the-Rol-Loo.

And neat little Titty-Fol-Leh
Was eaten by Pish-Pooh-Bah,
And light-hearted Waggety-Weh
By dismal Alack-a-Deh-Ah—
Despairing Alack-a-Deh-Ah.

And rollicking Tral-the-Ral-Lah
Was eaten by Doodle-Dum-Deh,
And musical Doh-Reh-Mi-Fah
By good little Tootle-Tum-Teh—
Exemplary Tootle-Tum-Teh!

THE TROUBADOUR.

A troubadour he played
Without a castle wall,
Within, a hapless maid
Responded to his call.

"Oh, willow, woe is me!
Alack and well-a-day!
If I were only free
I'd hie me far away!"

Unknown her face and name,
But this he knew right well,
The maiden's wailing came
From out a dungeon cell.

A hapless woman lay
Within that dungeon grim—
That fact, I've heard him say.
Was quite enough for him.

"I will not sit or lie,
Or eat or drink, I vow.
Till thou art free as I,
Or I as pent as thou."

Her tears then ceased to flow,
Her wails no longer rang,
And tuneful in her woe
The prisoned maiden sang:

"Oh, stranger, as you play
I recognize your touch;
And all that I can say
Is, thank you very much."

He seized his clarion straight,
And blew thereat, until
A warden oped the gate,
"Oh, what might be your will?"

"I've come, sir knave, to see
The master of these halls:
A maid unwillingly

Lies prisoned in their walls."

With barely stifled sigh
That porter drooped his head,
With teardrops in his eye,
"A many, sir," he said.

He stayed to hear no more,
But pushed that porter by,
And shortly stood before
Sir Hugh de Peckham Rye.

Sir Hugh he darkly frowned,
"What would you, sir, with me?"
The troubadour he downed
Upon his bended knee.

"I've come, De Peckham Rye,
To do a Christian task;
You ask me what would I?
It is not much I ask.

"Release these maidens, sir,
Whom you dominion o'er—
Particularly her
Upon the second floor.

"And if you don't, my lord"—
He here stood bolt upright,
And tapped a tailor's sword—
"Come out, you cad, and fight!"

Sir Hugh he called—and ran
The warden from the gate:
"Go, show this gentleman
The maid in forty-eight."

By many a cell they past,
And stopped at length before
A portal, bolted fast:
The man unlocked the door.

He called inside the gate
With coarse and brutal shout,
"Come, step it, Forty-eight!"
And Forty-eight stepped out.

"They gets it pretty hot,
The maidens what we cotch—
Two years this lady's got
For collaring a wotch."

"Oh, ah!—indeed—I see,"

The troubadour exclaimed—
"If I may make so free,
How is this castle named?"

The warden's eyelids fill,
And sighing, he replied,
"Of gloomy Pentonville
This is the female side!"

The minstrel did not wait
The warden stout to thank,
But recollected straight
He'd business at the Bank.

THE FORCE OF ARGUMENT.

Lord B. was a nobleman bold,
Who came of illustrious stocks,
He was thirty or forty years old,
And several feet in his socks.

To Turniptopville-by-the-Sea
This elegant nobleman went,
For that was a borough that he
Was anxious to rep-per-re-sent.

At local assemblies he danced
Until he felt thoroughly ill—
He waltzed, and he galloped, and lanced,
And threaded the mazy quadrille.

The maidens of Turniptopville
Were simple—ingenuous—pure—
And they all worked away with a will
The nobleman's heart to secure.

Two maidens all others beyond
Imagined their chances looked well—
The one was the lively Ann Pond,
The other sad Mary Morell.

Ann Pond had determined to try
And carry the Earl with a rush.
Her principal feature was eye,
Her greatest accomplishment—gush.

And Mary chose this for her play,
Whenever he looked in her eye
She'd blush and turn quickly away,
And flitter and flutter and sigh.

It was noticed he constantly sighed
As she worked out the scheme she had planned—
A fact he endeavored to hide
With his aristocratical hand.

Old Pond was a farmer, they say,
And so was old Tommy Morell,
In a humble and pottering way

They were doing exceedingly well.

They both of them carried by vote
The Earl was a dangerous man,
So nervously clearing his throat,
One morning old Tommy began:

"My darter's no pratty young doll —
I'm a plain-spoken Zommerzet man —
Now what do 'ee mean by my Poll,
And what do 'ee mean by his Ann?"

Said B., "I will give you my bond
I mean them uncommonly well,
Believe me, my excellent Pond,
And credit me, worthy Morell.

"It's quite indisputable, for
I'll prove it with singular ease,
You shall have it in 'Barbara' or
'Celarent' — whichever you please.

"You see, when an anchorite bows
To the yoke of intentional sin —
If the state of the country allows,
Homogeny always steps in.

"It's a highly æsthetical bond,
As any mere ploughboy can tell" —
"Of course," replied puzzled old Pond.
"I see," said old Tommy Morell.

"Very good then," continued the lord,
"When its fooled to the top of its bent,
With a sweep of a Damocles sword
The web of intention is rent.

"That's patent to all of us here,
As any mere schoolboy can tell."
Pond answered, "Of course it's quite clear;"
And so did that humbug Morell.

"It's tone esoteric in force —
I trust that I make myself clear?" —
Morell only answered "Of course," —
While Pond slowly muttered, "Hear, hear."

"Volition — celestial prize,
Pellucid as porphyry cell —
Is based on a principle wise."
"Quite so," exclaimed Pond and Morell.

"From what I have said, you will see

THE FORCE OF ARGUMENT.   31

That I couldn't wed either—in fine,
By nature's unchanging decree
Your daughters could never be *mine*.

"Go home to your pigs and your ricks,
My hands of the matter I've rinsed."
So they take up their hats and their sticks,
And *exeunt ambo*, convinced.

ONLY A DANCING GIRL.

Only a dancing girl,
With an unromantic style,
With borrowed color and curl,
With fixed mechanical smile,
With many a hackneyed wile,
With ungrammatical lips,
And corns that mar her trips!

Hung from the "flies" in air,
She acts a palpable lie,
She's as little a fairy there
As unpoetical I!
I hear you asking, Why—
Why in the world I sing

ONLY A DANCING GIRL.

This tawdry, tinselled thing?

No airy fairy she,
As she hangs in arsenic green,
From a highly impossible tree,
In a highly impossible scene
(Herself not over clean).
For fays don't suffer, I'm told,
From bunions, coughs, or cold.

And stately dames that bring
Their daughters there to see,
Pronounce the "dancing thing"
No better than she should be.
With her skirt at her shameful knee,
And her painted, tainted phiz:
Ah, matron, which of us is?

(And, in sooth, it oft occurs
That while these matrons sigh,
Their dresses are lower than hers,
And sometimes half as high;
And their hair is hair they buy,
And they use their glasses, too,
In a way she'd blush to do.)

But change her gold and green
For a coarse merino gown,
And see her upon the scene
Of her home, when coaxing down
Her drunken father's frown,
In his squalid, cheerless den:
She's a fairy truly, then!

THE SENSATION CAPTAIN.

No nobler captain ever trod
Than Captain Parklebury Todd,
So good—so wise—so brave, he!
But still, as all his friends would own,
He had one folly—one alone—
This Captain in the Navy.

I do not think I ever knew
A man so wholly given to
Creating a sensation;
Or p'r'aps I should in justice say—
To what in an Adelphi play
Is known as "Situation."

He passed his time designing traps
To flurry unsuspicious chaps—
The taste was his innately—
He couldn't walk into a room
Without ejaculating "Boom!"
Which startled ladies greatly.

He'd wear a mask and muffling cloak,
Not, you will understand, in joke,
As some assume disguises.
He did it, actuated by
A simple love of mystery
And fondness for surprises.

I need not say he loved a maid—
His eloquence threw into shade
All others who adored her:
The maid, though pleased at first, I know,
Found, after several years or so,
Her startling lover bored her.

So, when his orders came to sail,
She did not faint or scream or wail,
Or with her tears anoint him.
She shook his hand, and said "Good-bye;"
With laughter dancing in her eye—
Which seemed to disappoint him.

THE SENSATION CAPTAIN.

But ere he went aboard his boat
He placed around her little throat
A ribbon blue and yellow,
On which he hung a double tooth—
A simple token this, in sooth—
'Twas all he had, poor fellow!

"I often wonder," he would say,
When very, very far away,
"If Angelina wears it!
A plan has entered in my head,
I will pretend that I am dead,
And see how Angy bears it!"

The news he made a messmate tell:
His Angelina bore it well,
No sign gave she of crazing;
But, steady as the Inchcape rock
His Angelina stood the shock
With fortitude amazing.

She said, "Some one I must elect
Poor Angelina to protect
From all who wish to harm her.
Since worthy Captain Todd is dead
I rather feel inclined to wed
A comfortable farmer."

A comfortable farmer came
(Bassanio Tyler was his name)
Who had no end of treasure:
He said, "My noble gal, be mine!"
The noble gal did not decline,
But simply said, "With pleasure."

When this was told to Captain Todd,
At first he thought it rather odd,
And felt some perturbation;
But very long he did not grieve,
He thought he could a way perceive
To *such* a situation!

"I'll not reveal myself," said he,
"Till they are both in the Eccle-
siastical Arena;
Then suddenly I will appear,
And paralyzing them with fear,
Demand my Angelina!"

At length arrived the wedding day—
Accoutred in the usual way

Appeared the bridal body—
The worthy clergyman began,
When in the gallant captain ran
And cried, "Behold your Toddy!"

The bridegroom, p'r'aps, was terrified,
And also possibly the bride—
The bridesmaids *were* affrighted;
But Angelina, noble soul,
Contrived her feelings to control,
And really seemed delighted.

"My bride!" said gallant Captain Todd,
"She's mine, uninteresting clod,
My own, my darling charmer!"
"Oh, dear," said she, "you're just too late,
I'm married to, I beg to state,
This comfortable farmer!"

"Indeed," the farmer said, "she's mine,
You've been and cut it far too fine!"
"I see," said Todd, "I'm beaten."
And so he went to sea once more,
"Sensation" he for aye forswore,
And married on her native shore
A lady whom he'd met before—
A lovely Otaheitan.

THE PERIWINKLE GIRL.

I've often thought that headstrong youths,
Of decent education,
Determine all-important truths
With strange precipitation.

The over-ready victims they,
Of logical illusions,
And in a self-assertive way
They jump at strange conclusions.

Now take my case: Ere sorrow could
My ample forehead wrinkle,
I had determined that I would
Not like to be a winkle.

"A winkle," I would oft advance
With readiness provoking,
"Can seldom flirt, and never dance
Or soothe his mind by smoking."

In short, I spurned the shelly joy,
And spoke with strange decision—
Men pointed to me as a boy
Who held them in derision.

But I was young—too young, by far—
Or I had been more wary,
I knew not then that winkles are
The stock-in-trade of Mary.

I had not seen her sunlight blithe
As o'er their shells it dances,
I've seen those winkles almost writhe
Beneath her beaming glances.

Of slighting all the winkly brood
I surely had been chary,
If I had known they formed the food
And stock-in-trade of Mary.

Both high and low and great and small
Fell prostrate at her tootsies,
They all were noblemen, and all

Had balances at Coutts's.

Dukes with the lovely maiden dealt,
Duke Bailey and Duke Humphy,
Who eat her winkles till they felt
Exceedingly uncomfy.

Duke Bailey greatest wealth computes,
And sticks, they say, at no-thing.
He wears a pair of golden boots
And silver underclothing.

Duke Humphy, as I understand.
Though mentally acuter,
His boots are only silver, and
His underclothing pewter.

A third adorer had the girl,
A man of lowly station—
A miserable grov'ling earl
Besought her approbation.

This humble cad she did refuse
With much contempt and loathing;
He wore a pair of leather shoes
And cambric underclothing!

"Ha! ha!" she cried, "Upon my word!
Well, really—come, I never!
Oh, go along, it's too absurd!
My goodness! Did you ever?

"Two dukes would make their Bowles a bride,
And from her foes defend her"—
"Well, not exactly that," they cried,
"We offer guilty splendor.

"We do not offer marriage rite,
So please dismiss the notion!"
"Oh, dear," said she, "that alters quite
The state of my emotion."

The earl he up and says, says he,
"Dismiss them to their orgies,
For I am game to marry thee
Quite reg'lar at St. George's."

He'd had, it happily befell,
A decent education;
His views would have befitted well
A far superior station.

His sterling worth had worked a cure,

THE PERIWINKLE GIRL.

She never heard him grumble;
She saw his soul was good and pure
Although his rank was humble.

Her views of earldoms and their lot,
All underwent expansion;
Come, Virtue in an earldom's cot!
Go, Vice in ducal mansion!

BOB POLTER.

Bob Polter was a navvy, and
His hands were coarse, and dirty too,
His homely face was rough and tanned,
His time of life was thirty-two.

He lived among a working clan
(A wife he hadn't got at all),
A decent, steady, sober man—
No saint, however—not at all.

He smoked, but in a modest way,
Because he thought he needed it;
He drank a pot of beer a day,
And sometimes he exceeded it.

At times he'd pass with other men
A loud convivial night or two,
With, very likely, now and then,
On Saturdays, a fight or two.

But still he was a sober soul,
A labor-never-shirking man,
Who paid his way—upon the whole
A decent English working man.

One day, when at the Nelson's Head,
(For which he may be blamed of you)
A holy man appeared and said,
"Oh, Robert, I'm ashamed of you."

He laid his hand on Robert's beer
Before he could drink up any,
And on the floor, with sigh and tear,
He poured the pot of "thruppenny."

"Oh, Robert, at this very bar,
A truth you'll be discovering,
A good and evil genius are
Around your noddle hovering.

"They both are here to bid you shun
The other one's society,
For Total Abstinence is one,

BOB POLTER.

The other Inebriety."

He waved his hand—a vapor came—
A wizard, Polter reckoned him:
A bogy rose and called his name,
And with his finger beckoned him.

The monster's salient points to sum,
His heavy breath was portery;
His glowing nose suggested rum;
His eyes were gin-and-wortery.

His dress was torn—for dregs of ale
And slops of gin had rusted it;
His pimpled face was wan and pale,
Where filth had not encrusted it.

"Come, Polter," said the fiend, "begin,
And keep the bowl a-flowing on—
A working-man needs pints of gin
To keep his clockwork going on."

Bob shuddered: "Ah, you've made a miss,
If you take me for one of you—
You filthy beast, get out of this—
Bob Polter don't want none of you."

The demon gave a drunken shriek
And crept away in stealthiness,
And lo, instead, a person sleek
Who seemed to burst with healthiness.

"In me, as your advisor hints,
Of Abstinence you have got a type—
Of Mr. Tweedle's pretty prints
I am the happy prototype.

"If you abjure the social toast,
And pipes, and such frivolities,
You possibly some day may boast
My prepossessing qualities!"

Bob rubbed his eyes, and made 'em blink,
"You almost make me tremble, you!
If I abjure fermented drink,
Shall I, indeed, resemble you?

"And will my whiskers curl so tight?
My cheeks grow smug and muttony?
My face become so red and white?
My coat so blue and buttony?

"Will trousers, such as yours, array

Extremities inferior?
Will chubbiness assert its sway
All over my exterior?

"In this, my unenlightened state,
To work in heavy boots I comes,
Will pumps henceforward decorate
My tiddle toddle tootsicums?

"And shall I get so plump and fresh,
And look no longer seedily?
My skin will henceforth fit my flesh
So tightly and so Tweedie-ly?"

The phantom said, "You'll have all this,
You'll know no kind of huffiness,
Your life will be one chubby bliss,
One long unruffled puffiness!"

"Be off!" said irritated Bob.
"Why come you here to bother one?
You pharisaical old snob,
You're wuss almost than t'other one!

"I takes my pipe—I takes my pot,
And drunk I'm never seen to be:
I'm no teetotaller or sot,
And as I am I mean to be!"

GENTLE ALICE BROWN.

It was a robber's daughter, and her name was Alice Brown;
Her father was the terror of a small Italian town;
Her mother was a foolish, weak, but amiable old thing;
But it isn't of her parents that I'm going for to sing.

As Alice was a-sitting at her window-sill one day,
A beautiful young gentleman he chanced to pass that way;
She cast her eyes upon him, and he looked so good and true,
That she thought, "I could be happy with a gentleman like you!"

And every morning passed her house that cream of gentlemen,
She knew she might expect him at a quarter unto ten,
A sorter in the Custom-house, it was his daily road
(The Custom-house was fifteen minutes' walk from her abode).

But Alice was a pious girl, who knew it wasn't wise

To look at strange young sorters with expressive purple eyes;
So she sought the village priest, to whom her family confessed,
The priest by whom their little sins were carefully assessed.

"Oh, holy father," Alice said, "'twould grieve you, would it not?
To discover that I was a most disreputable lot!
Of all unhappy sinners I'm the most unhappy one!"
The padre said, "Whatever have you been and gone and done?"

"I have helped mamma to steal a little kiddy from its dad,
I've assisted dear papa in cutting up a little lad,
I've planned a little burglary and forged a little check,
And slain a little baby for the coral on its neck!"

The worthy pastor heaved a sigh and dropped a silent tear—
And said, "You mustn't judge yourself too heavily, my dear—
It's wrong to murder babies, little corals for to fleece:
But sins like that one expiates at half-a-crown apiece.

"Girls will be girls—you're very young, and flighty in your mind;
Old heads upon young shoulders we must not expect to find;
We mustn't be too hard upon these little girlish tricks—
Let's see—five crimes at half-a-crown—exactly twelve-and-six."

"Oh, father," little Alice cried, "your kindness makes me weep,
You do these little things for me so singularly cheap—
Your thoughtful liberality I never can forget;
But, O, there is another crime I haven't mentioned yet!"

"A pleasant-looking gentleman, with pretty purple eyes,
I've noticed at my window, as I've sat a-catching flies:
He passes by it every day as certain as can be—
I blush to say I've winked at him and he has winked at me!"

"For shame," said Father Paul, "my erring daughter! On my word
This is the most distressing news that I have ever heard.
Why, naughty girl, your excellent papa has pledged your hand
To a promising young robber, the lieutenant of his band!

"This dreadful piece of news will pain your worthy parents so!
They are the most remunerative customers I know;
For many years they've kept starvation from my doors,
I never knew so criminal a family as yours!

"The common country folk in this insipid neighborhood
Have nothing to confess, they're so ridiculously good;
And if you marry any one respectable at all,
Why, you'll reform, and what will then become of Father Paul?"

The worthy priest, he up and drew his cowl upon his crown,
And started off in haste to tell the news to Robber Brown;
To tell him how his daughter, who now was for marriage fit,
Had winked upon a sorter, who reciprocated it.

GENTLE ALICE BROWN.

Good Robber Brown he muffled up his anger pretty well,
He said "I have a notion, and that notion I will tell;
I will nab this gay young sorter, terrify him into fits,
And get my gentle wife to chop him into little bits.

"I've studied human nature, and I know a thing or two,
Though a girl may fondly love a living gent, as many do—
A feeling of disgust upon her senses there will fall
When she looks upon his body chopped particularly small."

He traced that gallant sorter to a still suburban square;
He watched his opportunity and seized him unaware;
He took a life-preserver and he hit him on the head,
And Mrs. Brown dissected him before she went to bed.

And pretty little Alice grew more settled in her mind,
She never more was guilty of a weakness of the kind,
Until at length good Robber Brown bestowed her pretty hand
On the promising young robber, the lieutenant of his band.

BEN ALLAH ACHMET;
OR, THE FATAL TUM.

I once did know a Turkish man
Whom I upon a two-pair-back met,
His name it was Effendi Khan
Backsheesh Pasha Ben Allah Achmet.

A Doctor Brown I also knew—
I've often eaten of his bounty—
The Turk and he they lived at Hooe,
In Sussex, that delightful county.

I knew a nice young lady there,
Her name was Isabella Sherson,
And though she wore another's hair,
She was an interesting person.

The Turk adored the maid of Hooe
(Although his harem would have shocked her);
But Brown adored that maiden, too:
He was a most seductive doctor.

They'd follow her where'er she'd go—
A course of action most improper;
She neither knew by sight, and so
For neither of them cared a copper.

Brown did not know that Turkish male,
He might have been his sainted mother:
The people in this simple tale
Are total strangers to each other.

One day that Turk he sickened sore
Which threw him straight into a sharp pet;
He threw himself upon the floor
And rolled about upon his—carpet.

It made him moan—it made him groan
And almost wore him to a mummy:
Why should I hesitate to own
That pain was in his little tummy?

At length a Doctor came and rung

BEN ALLAH ACHMET;

(As Allah Achmet had desired)
Who felt his pulse, looked up his tongue,
And hummed and hawed, and then inquired:

"Where is the pain, that long has preyed
Upon you in so sad a way, sir?"
The Turk he giggled, blushed, and said,
"I don't exactly like to say, sir."

"Come, nonsense!" said good Doctor Brown,
"So this is Turkish coyness, is it?
You must contrive to fight it down—
Come, come, sir, please to be explicit."

The Turk he shyly bit his thumb,
And coyly blushed like one half-witted,
"The pain is in my little tum,"
He, whispering, at length admitted.

"Then take you this, and take you that—
Your blood flows sluggish in its channel—
You must get rid of all this fat,
And wear my medicated flannel.

"You'll send for me, when you're in need—
My name is Brown—your life I've saved it!"
"My rival!" shrieked the invalid,
And drew a mighty sword and waved it.

"This to thy weazand, Christian pest!"
Aloud the Turk in frenzy yelled it,
And drove right through the Doctor's chest
The sabre and the hand that held it.

The blow was a decisive one,
And Doctor Brown grew deadly pasty—
"Now see the mischief that you've done,—
You Turks are so extremely hasty.

"There are two Doctor Browns in Hooe,
He's short and stout—*I'm* tall and wizen;
You've been and run the wrong one through,
That's how the error has arisen."

The accident was thus explained,
Apologies were only heard now:
"At my mistake I'm really pained,
I am, indeed, upon my word now."

"With me, sir, you shall be interred,
A Mausoleum grand awaits me"—
"Oh, pray don't say another word,
I'm sure that more than compensates me.

"But, p'r'aps, kind Turk, you're full inside?"
"There's room," said he, "for any number."
And so they laid them down and died.
In proud Stamboul they sleep their slumber.

SONGS OF A SAVOYARD

THE ENGLISHMAN.

He is an Englishman!
For he himself has said it,
And it's greatly to his credit,
That he is an Englishman!
For he might have been a Roosian,
A French, or Turk, or Proosian,
Or perhaps Itali-an!
But in spite of all temptations,
To belong to other nations,
He remains an Englishman!
Hurrah!
For the true born Englishman!

THE DISAGREEABLE MAN.

If you give me your attention, I will tell you what I am:
I'm a genuine philanthropist—all other kinds are sham.
Each little fault of temper and each social defect
In my erring fellow creatures, I endeavor to correct.
To all their little weaknesses I open people's eyes
And little plans to snub the self-sufficient I devise;
I love my fellow creatures—I do all the good I can—
Yet everybody say I'm such a disagreeable man!
And I can't think why!

To compliments inflated I've a withering reply;
And vanity I always do my best to mortify;
A charitable action I can skilfully dissect:
And interested motives I'm delighted to detect.
I know everybody's income and what everybody earns,
And I carefully compare it with the income tax returns;
But to benefit humanity, however much I plan,
Yet everybody says I'm such a disagreeable man!
And I can't think why!

I'm sure I'm no ascetic: I'm as pleasant as can be;
You'll always find me ready with a crushing repartee;
I've an irritating chuckle; I've a celebrated sneer;
I've an entertaining snigger; I've a fascinating leer;
To everybody's prejudice I know a thing or two;
I can tell a woman's age in half a minute—and I do—
But although I try to make myself as pleasant as I can,
Yet everybody says I'm such a disagreeable man!
And I can't think why!

THE MODERN MAJOR-GENERAL.

I am the very pattern of a modern Major-Gineral.
I've information vegetable, animal, and mineral;
I know the kings of England, and I quote the fights historical,
From Marathon to Waterloo, in order categorical;
I'm very well acquainted too with matters mathematical,
I understand equations, both the simple and quadratical,
About binomial theorem I'm teeming with a lot o' news,
With many cheerful facts about the square of the hypotenuse.
I'm very good at integral and differential calculus,
I know the scientific names of beings animalculous,
In short in matters vegetable, animal and mineral,
I am the very model of a modern Major-Gineral.

I know our mythic history—King Arthur's and Sir Caradoc's,
I answer hard acrostics, I've a pretty taste for paradox,
I quote in elegiacs all the crimes of Heliogabalus,
In conies I can floor peculiarities parabolous.
I can tell undoubted Raphaels from Gerard Dows and Zoffanies,
I know the croaking chorus from the "Frogs" of Aristophanes,
Then I can hum a fugue of which I've heard the music's din afore,
And whistle all the airs from that confounded nonsense "Pinafore."
Then I can write a washing bill in Babylonic cuneiform,
And tell you every detail of Caractacus's uniform.
In short in matters vegetable, animal and mineral,
I am the very model of a modern Major-Gineral.

In fact when I know what is meant by "mamelon" and "ravelin,"
When I can tell at sight a Chassepot rifle from a javelin,
When such affairs as *sorties* and surprises I'm more wary at,
And when I know precisely what is meant by Commissariat,
When I have learn what progress has been made in modern gunnery,
When I know more of tactics than a novice in a nunnery,
In short when I've a smattering of elementary strategy,
You'll say a better Major-Gene*ral* has never *sat* a gee—
For my military knowledge, though I'm plucky and adventury,
Has only been brought down to the beginning of the century,

THE MODERN MAJOR-GENERAL.

But still in learning vegetable, animal and mineral,
I am the very model of a modern Major-Gineral.

THE HEAVY DRAGOON.

If you want a receipt for that popular mystery
Known to the world as a Heavy Dragoon,
Take all the remarkable people in history,
Rattle them off to a popular tune!
The pluck of Lord Nelson on board of the *Victory*—
Genius of Bismarck devising a plan;
The humor of Fielding (which sounds contradictory)—
Coolness of Paget about to trepan—
The grace of Mozart, that unparalleled musico—
Wit of Macaulay, who wrote of Queen Anne—
The pathos of Paddy, as rendered by Boucicault—
Style of the Bishop of Sodor and Man—
The dash of a D'Orsay, divested of quackery—
Narrative powers of Dickens and Thackeray
Victor Emmanuel—peak-haunting Peveril—
Thomas Aquinas, and Doctor Sacheverell—
Tupper and Tennyson—Daniel Defoe—
Anthony Trollope and Mister Guizot!

Take of these elements all that are fusible,
Melt them all down in a pipkin or crucible,
Set them to simmer and take off the scum,
And a Heavy Dragoon is the residuum!

If you want a receipt for this soldierlike paragon,
Get at the wealth of the Czar (if you can)—
The family pride of a Spaniard from Arragon—
Force of Mephisto pronouncing a ban—
A smack of Lord Waterford, reckless and rollicky—
Swagger of Roderick, heading his clan—
The keen penetration of Paddington Pollaky—
Grace of an Odalisque on a divan—
The genius strategic of Cæsar or Hannibal—
Skill of Lord Wolseley in thrashing a cannibal
Flavor of Hamlet—the Stranger, a touch of him—
Little of Manfred, (but not very much of him)—
Beadle of Burlington—Richardson's show;
Mr. Micawber and Madame Tussaud!

THE HEAVY DRAGOON.

Take of these elements all that are fusible,
Melt them all down in a pipkin or crucible,
Set them to simmer and take off the scum,
And a Heavy Dragoon is the residuum!

ONLY ROSES!

To a garden full of posies
Cometh one to gather flowers,
And he wanders through its bowers
Toying with the wanton roses,
Who, uprising from their beds,
Hold on high their shameless heads
With their pretty lips a-pouting,
Never doubting—never doubting
That for Cytherean posies
He would gather aught but roses!

In a nest of weeds and nettles,
Lay a violet, half hidden,
Hoping that his glance unbidden
Yet might fall upon her petals,
Though she lived alone, apart,
Hope lay nestling at her heart,
But, alas! the cruel awaking
Set her little heart a-breaking,
For he gathered for his posies
Only roses—only roses!

THEY'LL NONE OF 'EM BE MISSED.

As some day it may happen that a victim must be found,
I've got a little list—I've got a little list
Of social offenders who might well be underground,
And who never would be missed—who never would be missed!
There's the pestilential nuisances who write for autographs—
All people who have flabby hands and irritating laughs—
All children who are up in dates, and floor you with 'em flat—
All persons who in shaking hands, shake hands with you like *that*—
And all third persons who on spoiling *tete-a-tetes* insist—
They'd none of 'em be missed—they'd none of 'em be missed!

There's the nigger serenader, and the others of his race,
And the piano organist—I've got him on the list!
And the people who eat peppermint and puff it in your face,
They never would be missed—they never would be missed!
Then the idiot who praises, with enthusiastic tone,
All centuries but this, and every country but his own;
And the lady from the provinces, who dresses like a guy,
And who doesn't think she waltzes, but would rather like to try;
And that singular anomaly, the lady novelist—
I don't think she'd be missed—I'm *sure* she'd not be missed!

And that *Nisi Prius* nuisance, who just now is rather rife,
The Judicial humorist—I've got *him* on the list!
All funny fellows, comic men, and clowns of private life—
They'd none of 'em be missed—they'd none of them be missed.
And apologetic statesmen of the compromising kind,
Such as—What-d'ye-call-him—Thing'em-Bob, and likewise—Never-mind,
And 'St—'st—'st—and What's-his-name, and also—You-know-who—
(The task of filling up the blanks I'd rather leave to *you*!)
But it really doesn't matter whom you put upon the list,
For they'd none of 'em be missed—they'd none of 'em be missed!

THE POLICEMAN'S LOT.

When a felon's not engaged in his employment
Or maturing his felonious little plans.
His capacity for innocent enjoyment,
Is just as great as any honest man's
Our feelings we with difficulty smother
When constabulary duty's to be done:
Ah, take one consideration with another,
A policeman's lot is not a happy one!

When the enterprising burglar isn't burgling,
When the cut-throat isn't occupied in crime,
He loves to hear the little brook a-gurgling,
And listen to the merry village chime.
When the coster's finished jumping on his mother,
He loves to lie a-basking in the sun:
Ah, take one consideration with another,
The policeman's lot is not a happy one!

THE POLICEMAN'S LOT.

AN APPEAL.

Oh, is there not one maiden breast
Which does not feel the moral beauty
Of making worldly interest
Subordinate to sense of duly?
Who would not give up willingly
All matrimonial ambition,
To rescue such a one as I
From his unfortunate position?

Oh, is there not one maiden here,
Whose homely face and bad complexion
Have caused all hopes to disappear
Of ever winning man's affection?
To such a one, if such there be,
I swear by Heaven's arch above you,
If you will cast your eyes on me,—
However plain you be—I'll love you!

EHEU FUGACES—!

The air is charged with amatory numbers—
Soft madrigals, and dreamy lovers' lays.
Peace, peace, old heart! Why waken from its slumbers
The aching memory of the old, old days?

Time was when Love and I were well acquainted.
Time was when we walked ever hand in hand;
A saintly youth, with worldly thought untainted,
None better-loved than I in all the land!
Time was, when maidens of the noblest station,
Forsaking even military men,
Would gaze upon me, rapt in adoration—
Ah, me, I was a fair young curate then!

Had I a headache? sighed the maids assembled;
Had I a cold? welled forth the silent tear;
Did I look pale? then half a parish trembled;
And when I coughed all thought the end was near!
I, had no care—no jealous doubts hung o'er me—
For I was loved beyond all other men.
Fled gilded dukes and belted earls before me!
Ah, me! I was a pale young curate then!

A RECIPE.

Take a pair of sparkling eyes,
Hidden, ever and anon,
In a merciful eclipse—
Do not heed their mild surprise—
Having passed the Rubicon.
Take a pair of rosy lips;
Take a figure trimly planned—
Such as admiration whets
(Be particular in this);
Take a tender little hand,
Fringed with dainty fingerettes,
Press it—in parenthesis;—
Take all these, you lucky man—
Take and keep them, if you can.

Take a pretty little cot—
Quite a miniature affair—
Hung about with trellised vine,
Furnish it upon the spot
With the treasures rich and rare
I've endeavored to define.
Live to love and love to live
You will ripen at your ease,
Growing on the sunny side—
Fate has nothing more to give.
You're a dainty man to please
If you are not satisfied.
Take my counsel, happy man:
Act upon it, if you can!

THE FIRST LORD'S SONG.

When I was a lad I served a term
As office boy to an Attorney's firm.
I cleaned the windows and I swept the floor,
And I polished up the handle of the big front door.
I polished up that handle so successfullee
That now I am the Ruler of the Queen's Navee!

As office boy I made such a mark
That they gave me the post of a junior clerk.
I served the writs with a smile so bland,
And I copied all the letters in a big round hand.
I copied all the letters in a hand so free,
That now I am the Ruler of the Queen's Navee!

In serving writs I made such a name
That an articled clerk I soon became;
I wore clean collars and a brand-new suit
For the Pass Examination at the Institute.
And that Pass Examination did so well for me,
That now I am the Ruler of the Queen's Navee!

Of legal knowledge I acquired such a grip
That they took me into the partnership.
And that junior partnership, I ween,
Was the only ship that I ever had seen,
But that kind of ship so suited me,
That now I am the Ruler of the Queen's Navee!

I grew so rich that I was sent
By a pocket borough into Parliament.
I always voted at my party's call,
And I never thought of thinking for myself at all.
I thought so little, they rewarded me,
By making me the Ruler of the Queen's Navee!

Now, landsmen all, whoever you may be,
If you want to rise to the top of the tree,
If your soul isn't fettered to an office stool,
Be careful to be guided by this golden rule—
Stick close to your desks and *never go to sea*,
And you all may be Rulers of the Queen's Navee!

WHEN A MERRY MAIDEN MARRIES.

When a merry maiden marries,
Sorrow goes and pleasure tarries;
Every sound becomes a song,
All is right and nothing's wrong!
From to-day and ever after
Let your tears be tears of laughter—
Every sigh that finds a vent
Be a sigh of sweet content!
When you marry merry maiden,
Then the air with love is laden;
Every flower is a rose,
Every goose becomes a swan,
Every kind of trouble goes
Where the last year's snows have gone!
Sunlight takes the place of shade
When you marry merry maid!

When a merry maiden marries
Sorrow goes and pleasure tarries;
Every sound becomes a song,
All is right, and nothing's wrong.
Gnawing Care and aching Sorrow,
Get ye gone until to-morrow;
Jealousies in grim array,
Ye are things of yesterday!
When you marry merry maiden,
Then the air with joy is laden;
All the corners of the earth
Ring with music sweetly played,
Worry is melodious mirth.
Grief is joy in masquerade;
Sullen night is laughing day—
All the year is merry May!

THE SUICIDE'S GRAVE.

On a tree by the river a little tomtit
Sang "Willow, titwillow, titwillow!"
And I said to him, "Dicky-bird, why do you sit
Singing 'Willow, titwillow, titwillow?'
Is it weakness of intellect, birdie?" I cried,
"Or a rather tough worm in your little inside?"
With a shake of his poor little head he replied,
"Oh, willow, titwillow, titwillow!"

He slapped at his chest, as he sat on that bough,
Singing "Willow, titwillow, titwillow!"
And a cold perspiration bespangled his brow,
Oh, willow, titwillow, titwillow!
He sobbed and he sighed, and a gurgle he gave,
Then he threw himself into the billowy wave,
And an echo arose from the suicide's grave—
"Oh, willow, titwillow, titwillow!"

Now I feel just as sure as I'm sure that my name
Isn't Willow, titwillow, titwillow,
That 'twas blighted affection that made him exclaim,
"Oh, willow, titwillow, titwillow!"
And if you remain callous and obdurate, I
Shall perish as he did, and you will know why,
Though I probably shall not exclaim as I die,
"Oh, willow, titwillow, titwillow!"

HE AND SHE.

HE.

I know a youth who loves a little maid—
(Hey, but his face is a sight for to see!)
Silent is he, for he's modest and afraid—
(Hey, but he's timid as a youth can be!)

SHE.

I know a maid who loves a gallant youth,
(Hey, but she sickens as the days go by!)
She cannot tell him all the sad, sad truth—
(Hey, but I think that little maid will die!)

BOTH.

Now tell me pray, and tell me true,
What in the world should the poor soul do?

HE.

He cannot eat and he cannot sleep—
(Hey, but his face is a sight for to see!)
Daily he goes for to wail—for to weep—
(Hey, but he's wretched as a youth can be!)

SHE.

She's very thin and she's very pale—
(Hey, but she sickens as the days go by!)
Daily she goes for to weep—for to wail—
(Hey, but I think that little maid will die!)

BOTH.

Now tell me pray, and tell me true,
What in the world should the poor soul do?

SHE.

If I were the youth I should offer her my name—
(Hey, but her face is a sight for to see!)

HE AND SHE.

HE.

If I were the maid I should feed his honest flame—
(Hey, but he's bashful as a youth can be!)

SHE.

If I were the youth I should speak to her to-day—
(Hey, but she sickens as the days go by!)

HE.

If I were the maid I should meet the lad half way—
(For I really do believe that timid youth will die'!)

BOTH.

I thank you much for your counsel true;
I've learnt what that poor soul ought to do!

THE LORD CHANCELLOR'S SONG.

The law is the true embodiment
Of everything that's excellent.
It has no kind of fault or flaw,
And I, my lords, embody the Law.
The constitutional guardian I
Of pretty young Wards in Chancery,
All very agreeable girls—and none
Are over the age of twenty-one.
A pleasant occupation for
A rather susceptible Chancellor!

But though the compliment implied
Inflates me with legitimate pride,
It nevertheless can't be denied
That it has its inconvenient side.
For I'm not so old, and not so plain,
And I'm quite prepared to marry again,
But there'd be the deuce to pay in the Lords
If I fell in love with one of my Wards:
Which rather tries my temper, for
I'm *such* a susceptible Chancellor!

THE LORD CHANCELLOR'S SONG.

And everyone who'd marry a Ward
Must come to me for my accord:
So in my court I sit all day,
Giving agreeable girls away,
With one for him—and one for he—
And one for you—and one for ye—
And one for thou—and one for thee—
But never, oh never a one for me!
Which is exasperating, for
A highly susceptible Chancellor!

WILLOW WALY!

HE.

Prithee, pretty maiden—prithee, tell me true
(Hey, but I'm doleful, willow, willow waly!)
Have you e'er a lover a-dangling after you?
Hey, willow waly O!
I fain would discover
If you have a lover?
Hey, willow waly O!

SHE.

Gentle sir, my heart is frolicsome and free—
(Hey but he's doleful, willow, willow waly!)
Nobody I care for comes a-courting me—
Hey, willow waly O!
Nobody I care for
Comes a-courting—therefore,
Hey, willow waly O!

HE.

Prithee, pretty maiden, will you marry me?
(Hey, but I'm hopeful, willow, willow waly!)
I may say, at once, I'm a man of propertee
Hey, willow waly O!
Money, I despise it,
But many people prize it,
Hey, willow waly O!

SHE.

Gentle sir, although to marry I design—
(Hey, but I'm hopeful, willow, willow waly!)
As yet I do not know you, and so I must decline.
Hey, willow waly O!
To other maidens go you—
As yet I do not know you,
Hey, willow waly O!

THE USHER'S CHARGE.

Now, Jurymen, hear my advice—
All kinds of vulgar prejudice
I pray you set aside:
With stern judicial frame of mind,
From bias free of every kind,
This trial must be tried!

Oh, listen to the plaintiff's case:
Observe the features of her face—
The broken-hearted bride!
Condole with her distress of mind:
From bias free of every kind,
This trial must be tried!

And when amid the plaintiff's shrieks,
The ruffianly defendant speaks—
Upon the other side;
What *he* may say you needn't mind—
From bias free of every kind,
This trial must be tried!

KING GOODHEART.

There lived a King, as I've been told,
In the wonder-working days of old,
When hearts were twice as good as gold,
And twenty times as mellow.
Good temper triumphed in his face,
And in his heart he found a place
For all the erring human race
And every wretched fellow.
When he had Rhenish wine to drink
It made him very sad to think
That some, at junket or at jink,
Must be content with toddy.
He wished all men as rich as he
(And he was rich as rich could be),
So to the top of every tree
Promoted everybody.

Ambassadors cropped up like hay,
Prime Ministers and such as they
Grew like asparagus in May,
And Dukes were three a penny.
Lord Chancellors were cheap as sprats.
And Bishops in their shovel hats
Were plentiful as tabby cats—
If possible, too many.
On every side Field-Marshals gleamed,
Small beer were Lords Lieutenant deemed
With Admirals the ocean teemed
All round his wide dominions;
And Party Leaders you might meet
In twos and threes in every street
Maintaining, with no little heat,
Their various opinions.

That King, although no one denies
His heart was of abnormal size,
Yet he'd have acted otherwise
If he had been acuter.
The end is easily foretold,

KING GOODHEART.

When every blessed thing you hold
Is made of silver, or of gold,
You long for simple pewter.
When you have nothing else to wear
But cloth of gold and satins rare,
For cloth of gold you cease to care—
Up goes the price of shoddy.
In short, whoever you may be,
To this conclusion you'll agree,
When every one is somebodee,
Then no one's anybody!

THE TANGLED SKEIN.

Try we life long, we can never
Straighten out life's tangled skein,
Why should we, in vain endeavor,
Guess and guess and guess again?
Life's a pudding full of plums;
Care's a canker that benumbs.
Wherefore waste our elocution
On impossible solution?
Life's a pleasant institution,
Let us take it as it comes!

Set aside the dull enigma,
We shall guess it all too soon;
Failure brings no kind of stigma—
Dance we to another tune!
String the lyre and fill the cup,
Lest on sorrow we should sup.
Hop and skip to Fancy's fiddle,
Hands across and down the middle—
Life's perhaps the only riddle
That we shrink from giving up!

GIRL GRADUATES.

They intend to send a wire
To the moon;
And they'll set the Thames on fire
Very soon;
Then they learn to make silk purses
With their rigs
From the ears of Lady Circe's
Piggy-wigs.
And weazels at their slumbers
They'll trepan;
To get sunbeams from cu*cum*bers
They've a plan.
They've a firmly rooted notion
They can cross the Polar Ocean,
And they'll find Perpetual Motion
If they can!

These are the phenomena
That every pretty domina
Hopes that we shall see
At this Universitee!

As for fashion, they forswear it,
So they say,
And the circle—they will square it
Some fine day;
Then the little pigs they're teaching
For to fly;
And the niggers they'll be bleaching
Bye and bye!
Each newly joined aspirant
To the clan
Must repudiate the tyrant
Known as Man;
They mock at him and flout him,
For they do not care about him,
And they're "going to do without him"
If they can!

These are the phenomena
That every pretty domina
Hopes that we shall see
At this Universitee!

THE APE AND THE LADY.

A lady fair, of lineage high,
Was loved by an Ape, in the days gone by—
The Maid was radiant as the sun,
The Ape was a most unsightly one—
So it would not do—
His scheme fell through;
For the Maid, when his love took formal shape,
Expressed such terror
At his monstrous error,
That he stammered an apology and made his 'scape,
The picture of a disconcerted Ape.

With a view to rise in the social scale,
He shaved his bristles, and he docked his tail,
He grew moustachios, and he took his tub,
And he paid a guinea to a toilet club.
But it would not do,
The scheme fell through—
For the Maid was Beauty's fairest Queen
With golden tresses,
Like a real princess's,
While the Ape, despite his razor keen,
Was the apiest Ape that ever was seen!

He bought white ties, and he bought dress suits,
He crammed his feet into bright tight boots,
And to start his life on a brand-new plan,
He christened himself Darwinian Man!
But it would not do.
The scheme fell through—
For the Maiden fair, whom the monkey craved,
Was a radiant Being,
With a brain far-seeing—
While a Man, however well-behaved,
At best is only a monkey shaved!

SANS SOUCI

I cannot tell what this love may be
That cometh to all but not to me.
It cannot be kind as they'd imply,
Or why do these gentle ladies sigh?
It cannot be joy and rapture deep,
Or why do these gentle ladies weep?
It cannot be blissful, as 'tis said,
Or why are their eyes so wondrous red?

If love is a thorn, they show no wit
Who foolishly hug and foster it.
If love is a weed, how simple they
Who gather and gather it, day by day!
If love is a nettle that makes you smart,
Why do you wear it next your heart?
And if it be neither of these, say I,
Why do you sit and sob and sigh?

THE BRITISH TAR.

A British tar is a soaring soul,
As free as a mountain bird,
His energetic fist should be ready to resist
A dictatorial word
His nose should pant and his lips should curl,
His cheeks should flame and his brow should furl,
His bosom should heave and his heart should glow,
And his fist be ever ready for a knock-down blow.

His eyes should flash with an inborn fire,
His brow with scorn be rung;
He never should bow down to a domineering frown,
Or the tang of a tyrant tongue.
His foot should stamp and his throat should growl,
His hair should twirl and his face should scowl:
His eyes should flash and his breast protrude,
And this should be his customary attitude!

THE COMING BYE AND BYE.

Sad is that woman's lot who, year by year,
Sees, one by one, her beauties disappear;
As Time, grown weary of her heart-drawn sighs,
Impatiently begins to "dim her eyes!"
Herself compelled, in life's uncertain gloamings,
To wreathe her wrinkled brow with well saved "combings"—
Reduced, with rouge, lipsalve, and pearly grey,
To "make up" for lost time, as best she may!

Silvered is the raven hair,
Spreading is the parting straight,
Mottled the complexion fair,
Halting is the youthful gait.
Hollow is the laughter free,
Spectacled the limpid eye,
Little will be left of me,

THE COMING BYE AND BYE.

In the coming bye and bye!

Fading is the taper waist—
Shapeless grows the shapely limb,
And although securely laced,
Spreading is the figure trim!
Stouter than I used to be,
Still more corpulent grow I—
There will be too much of me
In the coming bye and bye!

THE SORCERER'S SONG.

Oh! my name is John Wellington Wells—
I'm a dealer in magic and spells,
In blessings and curses,
And ever filled purses,
In prophecies, witches and knells!
If you want a proud foe to "make tracks"—
If you'd melt a rich uncle in wax—
You've but to look in
On our resident Djinn,
Number seventy, Simmery Axe.

We've a first class assortment of magic;
And for raising a posthumous shade
With effects that are comic or tragic,
There's no cheaper house in the trade.
Love-philtre—we've quantities of it;
And for knowledge if any one burns,
We keep an extremely small prophet, a prophet
Who brings us unbounded returns:
For he can prophesy
With a wink *of* his eye,
Peep with security
Into futurity,
Sum up your history,
Clear up a mystery,
Humor proclivity
For a nativity.
With mirrors so magical,
Tetrapods tragical,
Bogies spectacular,
Answers oracular,
Facts astronomical,
Solemn or comical,
And, if you want it, he
Makes a reduction on taking a quantity!
Oh!
If any one anything lacks,
He'll find it all ready in stacks,

THE SORCERER'S SONG.

If he'll only look in
On the resident Djinn,
Number seventy, Simmery Axe!

He can raise you hosts
Of ghosts,
And that without reflectors;
And creepy things
With wings,
And gaunt and grisly spectres!
He can fill you crowds
Of shrouds,
And horrify you vastly;
He can rack your brains
With chains,
And gibberings grim and ghastly.
Then, if you plan it, he
Changes organity,
With an urbanity,
Full of Satanity,
Vexes humanity
With an inanity
Fatal to vanity —
Driving your foes to the verge of insanity!
Barring tautology,
In demonology,
'Lectro biology,
Mystic nosology,
Spirit philology,
High class astrology,
Such is his knowledge, he
Isn't the man to require an apology!
Oh!
My name is John Wellington Wells,
I'm a dealer in magic and spells,
In blessings and curses,
And ever filled purses
In prophecies, witches and knells!
If any one anything lacks,
He'll find it all ready in stacks,
If he'll only look in
On the resident Djinn,
Number seventy, Simmery Axe!

SPECULATION.

Comes a train of little ladies
From scholastic trammels free,
Each a little bit afraid is,
Wondering what the world can be!

Is it but a world of trouble—
Sadness set to song?
Is its beauty but a bubble
Bound to break ere long?

Are its palaces and pleasures
Fantasies that fade?
And the glories of its treasures
Shadow of a shade?

Schoolgirls we, eighteen and under,
From scholastic trammels free,
And we wonder—how we wonder!—
What on earth the world can be!

THE DUKE OF PLAZA-TORO.

In enterprise of martial kind,
When there was any fighting,
He led his regiment from behind,
He found it less exciting.
But when away his regiment ran,
His place was at the fore, O—
That celebrated,
Cultivated,
Underrated
Nobleman,
The Duke of Plaza-Toro!
In the first and foremost flight, ha, ha!
You always found that knight, ha, ha!
That celebrated,
Cultivated,
Underrated
Nobleman,
The Duke of Plaza-Toro!

When, to evade Destruction's hand,
To hide they all proceeded,
No soldier in that gallant band
Hid half as well as he did.
He lay concealed throughout the war,
And so preserved his gore, O!
That unaffected,
Undetected,
Well connected
Warrior,
The Duke of Plaza-Toro!
In every doughty deed, ha ha!
He always took the lead, ha ha!
That unaffected,
Undetected,
Well connected
Warrior,
The Duke of Plaza-Toro!

When told that they would all be shot

Unless they left the service,
The hero hesitated not,
So marvellous his nerve is.
He sent his resignation in,
The first of all his corps, O!
That very knowing,
Overflowing,
Easy-going
Paladin,
The Duke of Plaza-Toro!
To men of grosser clay, ha, ha!
He always showed the way, ha, ha!
That very knowing,
Overflowing,
Easy-going
Paladin,
The Duke of Plaza-Toro!

THE REWARD OF MERIT.

Dr. Belville was regarded as the Crichton of his age:
His tragedies were reckoned much too thoughtful for the stage;
His poems held a noble rank, although it's very true
That, being very proper, they were read by very few.
He was a famous Painter, too, and shone upon the "line,"
And even Mr. Ruskin came and worshipped at his shrine;
But, alas, the school he followed was heroically high—
The kind of Art men rave about, but very seldom buy—
And everybody said
"How can he be repaid—
This very great—this very good—this very gifted man?"
But nobody could hit upon a practicable plan!

He was a great Inventor, and discovered, all alone,
A plan for making everybody's fortune but his own;
For, in business, an Inventor's little better than a fool,
And my highly gifted friend was no exception to the rule.
His poems—people read them in the Quarterly Reviews—
His pictures—they engraved them in the *Illustrated News*—
His inventions—they, perhaps, might have enriched him by degrees,
But all his little income went in Patent Office fees;
And everybody said
"How can he be repaid—
This very great—this very good—this very gifted man?"
But nobody could hit upon a practicable plan!

At last the point was given up in absolute despair,
When a distant cousin died, and he became a millionaire,
With a county seat in Parliament, a moor or two of grouse,
And a taste for making inconvenient speeches in the House!
Then it flashed upon Britannia that the fittest of rewards
Was, to take him from the Commons and to put him in the Lords!
And who so fit to sit in it, deny it if you can,
As this very great—this very good—this very gifted man?
(Though I'm more than half afraid
That it sometimes may be said
That we never should have revelled in that source of proper pride,
However great his merits—if his cousin hadn't died!)

WHEN I FIRST PUT THIS UNIFORM ON.

When I first put this uniform on,
I said as I looked in the glass.
"It's one to a million
That any civilian
My figure and form will surpass.
Gold lace has a charm for the fair,
And I've plenty of that, and to spare,
While a lover's professions,
When uttered in Hessians,
Are eloquent everywhere!
A fact that I counted upon,
When I first put this uniform on!"

I said, when I first put it on,
"It is plain to the veriest dunce
That every beauty
Will feel it her duty
To yield to its glamor at once.
They will see that I'm freely gold-laced
In a uniform handsome and chaste—
But the peripatetics
Of long-haired æsthetics,
Are very much more to their taste—
Which I never counted upon
When I first put this uniform on!"

SAID I TO MYSELF, SAID I.

When I went to the Bar as a very young man,
(Said I to myself—said I),
I'll work on a new and original plan
(Said I to myself—said I),
I'll never assume that a rogue or a thief
Is a gentleman worthy implicit belief,
Because his attorney has sent me a brief
(Said I to myself—said I!).

I'll never throw dust in a juryman's eyes
(Said I to myself—said I),
Or hoodwink a judge who is not over-wise
(Said I to myself—said I),
Or assume that the witnesses summoned in force
In Exchequer, Queen's Bench, Common Pleas, or Divorce,
Have perjured themselves as a matter of course
(Said I to myself—said I).

Ere I go into court I will read my brief through
(Said I to myself—said I),
And I'll never take work I'm unable to do
(Said I to myself—said I).

My learned profession I'll never disgrace
By taking a fee with a grin on my face,
When I haven't been there to attend to the case
(Said I to myself—said I!).

In other professions in which men engage
(Said I to myself—said I),
The Army, the Navy, the Church, and the Stage
(Said I to myself—said I),
Professional license, if carried too far,
Your chance of promotion will certainly mar
And I fancy the rule might apply to the Bar
(Said I to myself—said I!).

THE FAMILY FOOL.

Oh! a private buffoon is a light-hearted loon,
If you listen to popular rumor;
From morning to night he's so joyous and bright,
And he bubbles with wit and good-humor!
He's so quaint and so terse, both in prose and in verse;
Yet though people forgive his transgression,
There are one or two rules that all Family Fools
Must observe, if they love their profession.
There are one or two rules
Half a dozen, maybe,
That all family fools,
Of whatever degree,
Must observe, if they love their profession.

If you wish to succeed as a jester, you'll need
To consider each person auricular:
What is all right for B would quite scandalize C
(For C is so very particular);
And D may be dull, and E's very thick skull
Is as empty of brains as a ladle;
While F is F sharp, and will cry with a carp,
That he's known your best joke from his cradle!
When your humor they flout,
You can't let yourself go;
And it *does* put you out
When a person says, "Oh!
I have known that old joke from my cradle!"

If your master is surly, from getting up early
(And tempers are short in the morning),
An inopportune joke is enough to provoke
Him to give you, at once, a month's warning
Then if you refrain, he is at you again,
For he likes to get value for money.
He'll ask then and there, with an insolent stare,
If you know that you're paid to be funny?"
It adds to the task
Of a merryman's place,
When your principal asks,

With a scowl on his face,
If you know that you're paid to be funny?"

Comes a Bishop, maybe, or a solemn D.D.—
Oh, beware of his anger provoking!
Better not pull his hair—don't stick pins in his chair;
He don't understand practical joking.
If the jests that you crack have an orthodox smack,
You may get a bland smile from these sages;
But should it, by chance, be imported from France,
Half-a-crown is stopped out of your wages!
It's a general rule,
Though your zeal it may quench,
If the Family Fool
Makes a joke that's *too* French,
Half-a-crown is stopped out of his wages!

Though your head it may rack with a bilious attack,
And your senses with toothache you're losing,
Don't be mopy and flat—they don't fine you for that,
If you're properly quaint and amusing!
Though your wife ran away with a soldier that day,
And took with her your trifle of money;
Bless your heart, they don't mind—they're exceedingly kind—
They don't blame you—as long as you're funny!
It's a comfort to feel
If your partner should flit,
Though *you* suffer a deal,
They don't mind it a bit—
They don't blame you—so long as you're funny!

THE PHILOSOPHIC PILL.

I've wisdom from the East and from the West,
That's subject to no academic rule:
You may find it in the jeering of a jest,
Or distil it from the folly of a fool.
I can teach you with a quip, if I've a mind!
I can trick you into learning with a laugh;
Oh, winnow all my folly, and you'll find
A grain or two of truth among the chaff!

I can set a braggart quailing with a quip,
The upstart I can wither with a whim;
He may wear a merry laugh upon his lip,
But his laughter has an echo that is grim.
When they're offered to the world in merry guise,
Unpleasant truths are swallowed with a will—
For he who'd make his fellow creatures wise
Should always gild the philosophic pill!

THE CONTEMPLATIVE SENTRY.

When all night long a chap remains
On sentry-go, to chase monotony
He exercises of his brains,
That is, assuming that he's got any,
Though never nurtured in the lap
Of luxury, yet I admonish you,
I am an intellectual chap,
And think of things that would astonish you.
I often think it's comical
How Nature always does contrive
That every boy and every gal
That's born into the world alive
Is either a little Liberal,
Or else a little Conservative!
Fal lal la!

When in that house M.P.'s divide,
If they've a brain and cerebellum, too.
They're got to leave that brain outside.
And vote just as their leaders tell 'em to.
But then the prospect of a lot
Of statesmen, all in close proximity.
A-thinking for themselves, is what
No man can face with equanimity.
Then let's rejoice with loud Fal lal
That Nature wisely does contrive
That every boy and every gal
That's born into the world alive,
Is either a little Liberal,
Or else a little Conservative!
Fal lal la!

SORRY HER LOT.

Sorry her lot who loves too well,
Heavy the heart that hopes but vainly,
Had are the sighs that own the spell
Uttered by eyes that speak too plainly;
Heavy the sorrow that bows the head
When Love is alive and Hope is dead!

Sad is the hour when sets the Sun—
Dark is the night to Earth's poor daughters
When to the ark the wearied one
Flies from the empty waste of waters!
Heavy the sorrow that bows the head
When Love is alive and Hope is dead!

THE JUDGE'S SONG.

When I, good friends, was called to the Bar,
I'd an appetite fresh and hearty,
But I was, as many young barristers are,
An impecunious party.
I'd a swallow-tail coat of a beautiful blue—
A brief which I bought of a booby—
A couple of shirts and a collar or two,
And a ring that looked like a ruby!

In Westminster Hall I danced a dance,
Like a semi-despondent fury;
For I thought I should never hit on a chance
Of addressing a British Jury—
But I soon got tired of third class journeys,
And dinners of bread and water;
So I fell in love with a rich attorney's
Elderly, ugly daughter.

The rich attorney, he wiped his eyes,
And replied to my fond professions:
"You shall reap the reward of your enterprise,
At the Bailey and Middlesex Sessions.
You'll soon get used to her looks," said he,
"And a very nice girl you'll find her—
She may very well pass for forty-three
In the dusk, with a light behind her!"

The rich attorney was as good as his word:
The briefs came trooping gaily,
And every day my voice was heard
At the Sessions or Ancient Bailey.
All thieves who could my fees afford
Relied on my orations,
And many a burglar I've restored
To his friends and his relations.

At length I became as rich as the Gurneys—
An incubus then I thought her,
So I threw over that rich attorney's
Elderly, ugly daughter.

THE JUDGE'S SONG.

The rich attorney my character high
Tried vainly to disparage—
And now, if you please, I'm ready to try
This Breach of Promise of Marriage!

TRUE DIFFIDENCE.

My boy, you may take it from me,
That of all the afflictions accurst
With which a man's saddled
And hampered and addled,
diffident nature's the worst.
Though clever as clever can be—
A Crichton of early romance—
You must stir it and stump it,
And blow your own trumpet,
Or, trust me, you haven't a chance.

Now take, for example, *my* case:
I've a bright intellectual brain—
In all London city
There's no one so witty—
I've thought so again and again.
I've a highly intelligent face—
My features cannot be denied—
But, whatever I try, sir,
I fail in—and why, sir?
I'm modesty personified!

As a poet, I'm tender and quaint—
I've passion and fervor and grace—
From Ovid and Horace
To Swinburne and Morris,
They all of them take a back place,
Then I sing and I play and I paint;
Though none are accomplished as I,
To say so were treason:
You ask me the reason?
I'm diffident, modest and shy!

THE HIGHLY RESPECTABLE GONDOLIER.

I stole the Prince, and I brought him here,
And left him, gaily prattling
With a highly respectable Gondolier,
Who promised the Royal babe to rear,
And teach him the trade of a timoneer
With his own beloved bratling.

Both of the babes were strong and stout,
And, considering all things, clever.
Of that there is no manner of doubt—
No probable, possible shadow of doubt—
No possible doubt whatever.

Time sped, and when at the end of a year
I sought that infant cherished,
That highly respectable Gondolier
Was lying a corpse on his humble bier—
I dropped a Grand Inquisitor's tear—
That Gondolier had perished.

A taste for drink, combined with gout,
Had doubled him up for ever.
Of *that* there is no manner of doubt—
No probable, possible shadow of doubt—
No possible doubt whatever.

But owing, I'm much disposed to fear,
To his terrible taste for tippling,
That highly respectable Gondolier
Could never declare with a mind sincere
Which of the two was his offspring dear,
And which the Royal stripling!

Which was which he could never make out,
Despite his best endeavour.
Of *that* there is no manner of doubt—
No probable, possible shadow of doubt—
No possible doubt whatever.

The children followed his old career—
(This statement can't be parried)
Of a highly respectable Gondolier:
Well, one of the two (who will soon be here)—
But *which* of the two is not quite clear—
Is the Royal Prince you married!

Search in and out and round about
And you'll discover never
A tale so free from every doubt—
All probable, possible shadow of doubt—
All possible doubt whatever!

DON'T FORGET.

Now, Marco dear,
My wishes hear:
While you're away
It's understood
You will be good,
And not too gay.
To every trace
Of maiden grace
You will be blind,
And will not glance
By any chance
On womankind!
If you are wise,
You'll shut your eyes
'Till we arrive,
And not address
A lady less
Than forty-five;
You'll please to frown
On every gown
That you may see;
And O, my pet,
You won't forget
You've married me!

O, my darling, O, my pet,
Whatever else you may forget,
In yonder isle beyond the sea,
O, don't forget you've married me!

You'll lay your head
Upon your bed
At set of sun.
You will not sing
Of anything
To any one:
You'll sit and mope
All day, I hope,
And shed a tear

Upon the life
Your little wife
Is passing here!
And if so be
You think of me,
Please tell the moon:
I'll read it all
In rays that fall
On the lagoon:
You'll be so kind
As tell the wind
How you may be,
And send me words
By little birds
To comfort me!

And O, my darling, O, my pet,
Whatever else you may forget,
In yonder isle beyond the sea,
O, don't forget you've married me!

THE DARNED MOUNSEER.

I shipped, d'ye see, in a Revenue sloop,
And, off Cape Finistere,
A merchantman we see,
A Frenchman, going free,
So we made for the bold Mounseer.
D'ye see?
We made for the bold Mounseer!
But she proved to be a Frigate—and she up with her ports,
And fires with a thirty-two!
It come uncommon near,
But we answered with a cheer,
Which paralyzed the Parley-voo,
D'ye see?
Which paralyzed the Parley-voo!

Then our Captain he up and he says, says he,
"That chap we need not fear,—
We can take her, if we like,
She is sartin for to strike,
For she's only a darned Mounseer,
D'ye see?
She's only a darned Mounseer!
But to fight a French fal-lal—it's like hittin' of a gal—
It's a lubberly thing for to do;
For we, with all our faults,
Why, we're sturdy British salts,
While she's but a Parley-voo,
D'ye see?
A miserable Parley-voo!"

So we up with our helm, and we scuds before the breeze,
As we gives a compassionating cheer;
Froggee answers with a shout
As he sees us go about,
Which was grateful of the poor Mounseer,
D'ye see?
Which was grateful of the poor Mounseer!
And I'll wager in their joy they kissed each other's cheek
(Which is what them, furriners do),

And they blessed their lucky stars?
We were hardy British tars
Who had pity on a poor Parley-voo,
D'ye see?
Who had pity on a poor Parley-voo!

THE HUMANE MIKADO.

A more humane Mikado never
Did in Japan exist,
To nobody second,
I'm certainly reckoned
A true philanthropist,
It is my very humane endeavor
To make, to some extent,
Each evil liver
A running river
Of harmless merriment.
My object all sublime
I shall achieve in time—
To let the punishment fit the crime—
The punishment fit the crime;
And make each prisoner pent
Unwillingly represent
A source of innocent merriment,
Of innocent merriment!

All prosy dull society sinners,
Who chatter and bleat and bore,
Are sent to hear sermons
From mystical Germans
Who preach from ten to four,
The amateur tenor, whose vocal villanies
All desire to shirk,
Shall, during off hours,
Exhibit his powers
To Madame Tussaud's waxwork.
The lady who dyes a chemical yellow,
Or stains her grey hair puce,
Or pinches her figger,
Is blacked like a nigger
With permanent walnut juice.
The idiot who, in railway carriages,
Scribbles on window panes,
We only suffer
To ride on a buffer

In Parliamentary trains.
My object all sublime
I shall achieve in time—
To let the punishment fit the crime—
The punishment fit the crime;
And make each prisoner pent
Unwillingly represent
A source of innocent merriment,
Of innocent merriment!

The advertising quack who wearier
With tales of countless cures.
His teeth, I've enacted,
Shall all be extracted
By terrified amateurs.
The music hall singer attends a series
Of masses and fugues and "ops"
By Bach, interwoven
With Sophr and Beethoven,
At classical Monday Pops.
The billiard sharp whom any one catches,
His doom's extremely hard—
He's made to dwell
In a dungeon cell
On a spot that's always barred.
And there he plays extravagant matches
In fitless finger-stalls,
On a cloth untrue
With a twisted cue,
And elliptical billiard balls!

My object all sublime
I shall achieve in time—
To let the punishment fit the crime—
The punishment fit the crime;
And make each prisoner pent
Unwillingly represent
A source of innocent merriment,
Of innocent merriment!

THE HOUSE OF PEERS.

When Britain really ruled the waves—
(In good Queen Bess's time)
The House of Peers made no pretence
To intellectual eminence,
Or scholarship sublime;
Yet Britain won her proudest bays
In good Queen Bess's glorious days!

When Wellington thrashed Bonaparte,
As every child can tell,
The House of Peers, throughout the war,
Did nothing in particular,
And did it very well;
Yet Britain set the world a-blaze
In good King George's glorious days!

And while the House of Peers withholds
Its legislative hand.
And noble statesmen do not itch
To interfere with matters which
They do not understand,
As bright will shine Great Britain's rays,
As in King George's glorious days!

THE ÆSTHETE.

If you're anxious for to shine in the high æsthetic line, as a man of culture rare,
You must get up all the germs of the transcendental terms, and plant them everywhere.
You must lie upon the daisies and discourse in novel phrases of your complicated state of mind,
The meaning doesn't matter if it's only idle chatter of a transcendental kind.
And everyone will say,
As you walk your mystic way,
"If this young man expresses himself in terms too deep for *me*,
Why, what a very singularly deep young man this deep young man must be!"

Be eloquent in praise of the very dull old days which have long since passed away,
And convince 'em if you can, that the reign of good Queen Anne was Culture's palmiest day.
Of course you will pooh-pooh whatever's fresh and new, and

THE ÆSTHETE. 109

declare it's crude and mean,
And that art stopped short in the cultivated court of the Empress Josephine,
And everyone will say,
As you walk your mystic way,
"If that's not good enough for him which is good enough for *me*,
Why, what a very cultivated kind of youth this kind of youth must be!"

Then a sentimental passion of a vegetable fashion must excite your languid spleen,
An attachment *a la* Plato for a bashful young potato, or a not-too-French French bean.
Though the Philistines may jostle, you will rank as an apostle in the high æsthetic band,
If you walk down Picadilly with a poppy or a lily in your mediæval hand.
And everyone will say,
As you walk your flowery way,
"If he's content with a vegetable love which would certainly not suit *me*,
Why, what a most particularly pure young man this pure young man must be!"

PROPER PRIDE.

The Sun, whose rays
Are all ablaze
With ever living glory,
Does not deny
His majesty —
He scorns to tell a story!
He don't exclaim
"I blush for shame,
So kindly be indulgent,"
But, fierce and bold,
In fiery gold,
He glories all effulgent!

I mean to rule the earth.
As he the sky —
We really know our worth,
The Sun and I!

Observe his flame,
That placid dame,
The Moon's Celestial Highness;
There's not a trace
Upon her face
Of diffidence or shyness:
She borrows light
That, through the night,
Mankind may all acclaim her!
And, truth to tell,
She lights up well,
So I, for one, don't blame her!

Ah, pray make no mistake,
We are not shy;
We're very wide awake,
The Moon and I!

THE BAFFLED GRUMBLER.

Whene'er I poke
Sarcastic joke
Replete with malice spiteful,
The people vile
Politely smile
And vote me quite delightful!
Now, when a wight
Sits up all night
Ill-natured jokes devising,
And all his wiles
Are met with smiles,
It's hard, there's no disguising!
Oh, don't the days seem lank and long
When all goes right and nothing goes wrong,
And isn't your life extremely flat
With nothing whatever to grumble at!

When German bands
From music stands
Play Wagner imper*fect*ly—
I bid them go—
They don't say no,
But off they trot directly!
The organ boys
They stop their noise
With readiness surprising,
And grinning herds
Of hurdy-gurds
Retire apologizing!
Oh, don't the days seem lank and long
When all goes right and nothing goes wrong,
And isn't your life extremely flat
With nothing whatever to grumble at!

I've offered gold,
In sums untold,
To all who'd contradict me—
I've said I'd pay
A pound a day

To any one who kicked me—
I've bribed with toys
Great vulgar boys
To utter something spiteful,
But, bless you, no!
They *will* be so
Confoundedly politeful!
In short, these aggravating lads
They tickle my tastes, they feed my fads,
They give me this and they give me that,
And I've nothing whatever to grumble at!

THE WORKING MONARCH.

Rising early in the morning,
We proceed to light our fire;
Then our Majesty adorning
In its work-a-day attire,
We embark without delay
On the duties of the day.

First, we polish off some batches
Of political dispatches,
And foreign politicians circumvent;
Then, if business isn't heavy,
We may hold a Royal levee,
Or ratify some acts of Parliament;
Then we probably review the household troops—
With the usual "Shalloo humps!" and "Shalloo hoops!"
Or receive with ceremonial and state
An interesting Eastern Potentate,
After that we generally
Go and dress our private valet—
(It's rather a nervous duty—he's a touchy little man)
Write some letters literary
For our private secretary—
He is shaky in his spelling, so we help him if we can.
Then, in view of cravings inner,
We go down and order dinner;
Or we polish the Regalia and the Coronation Plate—
Spend an hour in titivating
All our Gentlemen-in-Waiting;
Or we run on little errands for the Ministers of State.
Oh, philosophers may sing
Of the troubles of a King;
Yet the duties are delightful, and the privileges great;
But the privilege and pleasure
That we treasure beyond measure
Is to run on little errands for the Ministers of State!

After luncheon (making merry
On a bun and glass of sherry),
If we've nothing particular to do,

We may make a Proclamation,
Or receive a Deputation—
Then we possibly create a Peer or two.
Then we help a fellow creature on his path
With the Garter or the Thistle or the Bath:
Or we dress and toddle off in semi-State
To a festival, a function, or a *fete*.
Then we go and stand as sentry
At the Palace (private entry),
Marching hither, marching thither, up and down and to and fro,
While the warrior on duty
Goes in search of beer and beauty
(And it generally happens that he hasn't far to go).
He relieves us, if he's able,
Just in time to lay the table,
Then we dine and serve the coffee; and at half-past twelve or one,
With a pleasure that's emphatic,
We retire to our attic
With the gratifying feeling that our duty has been done.
Oh, philosophers may sing
Of the troubles of a King,
But of pleasures there are many and of troubles there are none;
And the culminating pleasure
That we treasure beyond measure
Is the gratifying feeling that our duty has been done!

THE ROVER'S APOLOGY.

Oh, gentlemen, listen, I pray;
Though I own that my heart has been ranging,
Of nature the laws I obey,
For nature is constantly changing.
The moon in her phases is found,
The time and the wind and the weather,
The months in succession come round,
And you don't find two Mondays together.
Consider the moral, I pray,
Nor bring a young fellow to sorrow,
Who loves this young lady to-day,
And loves that young lady to-morrow.

You cannot eat breakfast all day,
Nor is it the act of a sinner,
When breakfast is taken away
To turn your attention to dinner;
And it's not in the range of belief,
That you could hold him as a glutton,
Who, when he is tired of beef,
Determines to tackle the mutton.
But this I am ready to say,
If it will diminish their sorrow,
I'll marry this lady to-day,
And I'll marry that lady to-morrow!

WOULD YOU KNOW?

Would you know the kind of maid
Sets my heart a flame-a?
Eyes must be downcast and staid,
Cheeks must flush for shame-a!
She may neither dance nor sing,
But, demure in everything,
Hang her head in modest way,
With pouting lips that seem to say
"Kiss me, kiss me, kiss me, kiss me,
Though I die of shame-a."
Please you, that's the kind of maid
Sets my heart a flame-a!

When a maid is bold and gay,
With a tongue goes clang-a,
Flaunting it in brave array,
Maiden may go hang-a!
Sunflower gay and hollyhock
Never shall my garden stock;
Mine the blushing rose of May,
With pouting lips that seem to say,
"Oh, kiss me, kiss me, kiss me, kiss me,
Though I die for shame-a!"
Please you, that's the kind of maid
Sets my heart a flame-a!

THE MAGNET AND THE CHURN.

A magnet hung in a hardware shop,
And all around was a loving crop
Of scissors and needles, nails and knives,
Offering love for all their lives;
But for iron the magnet felt no whim,
Though he charmed iron, it charmed not him,
From needles and nails and knives he'd turn,
For he'd set his love on a Silver Churn!
His most æsthetic,
Very magnetic
Fancy took this turn —
"If I can wheedle
A knife or needle,
Why not a Silver Churn?"

And Iron and Steel expressed surprise,
The needles opened their well drilled eyes,

The pen-knives felt "shut up," no doubt,
The scissors declared themselves "cut out."
The kettles they boiled with rage, 'tis said,
While every nail went off its head,
And hither and thither began to roam,
Till a hammer came up—and drove it home,
While this magnetic
Peripatetic
Lover he lived to learn,
By no endeavor,
Can Magnet ever
Attract a Silver Churn!

BRAID THE RAVEN HAIR.

Braid the raven hair,
Weave the supple tress,
Deck the maiden fair
In her loveliness;
Paint the pretty face,
Dye the coral lip.
Emphasize the grace
Of her ladyship!
Art and nature, thus allied,
Go to make a pretty bride!

Sit with downcast eye,
Let it brim with dew;
Try if you can cry,
We will do so, too.
When you're summoned, start
Like a frightened roe;
Flutter, little heart,
Color, come and go!
Modesty at marriage tide
Well becomes a pretty bride!

IS LIFE A BOON?

Is life a boon?
If so? it must befal
That Death, whene'er he call,
Must call too soon.
Though fourscore years he give,
Yet one would pray to live
Another moon!
What kind of plaint have I,
Who perish in July?
I might have had to die,
Perchance, in June!

Is life a thorn?
Then count it not a whit!
Man is well done with it;
Soon as he's born
He should all means essay
To put the plague away:
And I, war-worn,
Poor captured fugitive,
My life most gladly give —
I might have had to live
Another morn!

A MIRAGE.

Were I thy bride,
Then the whole world beside
Were not too wide
To hold my wealth of love —
Were I thy bride!
Upon thy breast
My loving head would rest,
As on her nest
The tender turtle dove —
Were I thy bride!

This heart of mine
Would be one heart with thine,
And in that shrine
Our happiness would dwell —
Were I thy bride!
And all day long
Our lives should be a song:
No grief, no wrong
Should make my heart rebel —
Were I thy bride!

The melancholy flute,
The melancholy lute,
Were night owl's hoot
To my low-whispered coo —
Were I thy bride!
The skylark's trill
Were but discordance shrill
To the soft thrill
Of wooing as I'd woo —
Were I thy bride!

The rose's sigh
Were as a carrion's cry
To lullaby
Such as I'd sing to thee,
Were I thy bride!
A feather's press

Were leaden heaviness
To my caress.
But then, unhappily,
I'm not thy bride!

A MERRY MADRIGAL.

Brightly dawns our wedding day;
Joyous hour, we give thee greeting!
Whither, whither art thou fleeting?
Fickle moment, prithee stay!
What though mortal joys be hollow?
Pleasures come, if sorrows follow:
Though the tocsin sound, ere long,
Ding dong! Ding dong!
Yet until the shadows fall
Over one and over all,
Sing a merry madrigal—
Fal la!

Let us dry the ready tear;
Though the hours are surely creeping,
Little need for woeful weeping,
Till the sad sundown is near.
All must sip the cup of sorrow—
I to-day and thou to-morrow:
This the close of every song—
Ding dong! Ding dong!
What, though solemn shadows fall,
Sooner, later, over all?
Sing a merry madrigal—
Fal la!

THE LOVE-SICK BOY.

When first my old, old love I knew,
My bosom welled with joy;
My riches at her feet I threw;
I was a love-sick boy!
No terms seemed too extravagant
Upon her to employ—
I used to mope, and sigh, and pant,
Just like a love-sick boy!

But joy incessant palls the sense;
And love, unchanged will cloy,
And she became a bore intense
Unto her love-sick boy!
With fitful glimmer burnt my flame,
And I grew cold and coy,
At last, one morning, I became
Another's love-sick boy!

Lector House believes that a society develops through a two-fold approach of continuous learning and adaptation, which is derived from the study of classic literary works spread across the historic timeline of literature records. Therefore, we aim at reviving, repairing and redeveloping all those inaccessible or damaged but historically as well as culturally important literature across subjects so that the future generations may have an opportunity to study and learn from past works to embark upon a journey of creating a better future.

This book is a result of an effort made by Lector House towards making a contribution to the preservation and repair of original ancient works which might hold historical significance to the approach of continuous learning across subjects.

HAPPY READING & LEARNING!

LECTOR HOUSE LLP
E-MAIL: lectorpublishing@gmail.com

www.ingramcontent.com/pod-product-compliance
Lightning Source LLC
LaVergne TN
LVHW042046070526
838201LV00078B/818